The Five-Ingredient Vegetarian Pressure Cooker Cookbook

The 5-Ingredient VEGETARIAN PRESSURE COOKER Cookbook

Fresh Pressure Cooker Recipes for Meals in Minutes

Jessica Harlan

ROCKRIDGE PRESS

For general information on our other products and services or to obtain technical support, please contact our Customer Care Department within the United States at (866) 744-2665, or outside the United States at (510) 253-0500.

Rockridge Press publishes its books in a variety of electronic and print formats. Some content that appears in print may not be available in electronic books, and vice versa.

Photography © Stockfood/Great Stock!, cover & p. 2; Stockfood/Elli Miller, p. 24; Stockfood/Brigitte Sporrer, p. 38; Stockfood/Zuzanna Ploch, p. 50 and back cover; Stocksy/Helen Rushbrook, pp. 72 & 84; Stockfood/Sporrer/ Skowronek, p. 100 and back cover; Stockfood/Amélie Roche, p. 120; Stockfood/Magdalena Hendey, p. 134; Stockfood/ Victoria Firmston, p. 148.

Print: 978-1-62-315872-9
Ebook: 978-1-62-315873-6

CONTENTS

7   Introduction

8   **CHAPTER ONE: THE BASICS**

23   **CHAPTER TWO: BUILDING BLOCKS**
25   Grains
39   Beans
51   Vegetables

71   **CHAPTER THREE: ONE-POT WONDERS**
73   Breakfasts
85   One-Pot Dinners
101 Soups and Stews

119 **CHAPTER FOUR: EXTRAS**
121 Desserts
135 Sauces and More

149 Conversion Tables
150 References
151 Recipe Index
153 Index
157 Recipe Label Index
161 About the Author

INTRODUCTION

IN THE FAST-PACED WORLD IN WHICH WE LIVE, doesn't it seem like there are never enough minutes in the day? Maybe you're a busy parent with a schedule chock-full of kids' activities and school events. Perhaps you have a demanding job with long hours and an onerous commute. Or maybe you just have an active social life and a long list of interests and hobbies.

If your busy schedule has trapped you into relying on ordering takeout, going through the drive-through, or microwaving a frozen dinner, the amazing abilities of an electric pressure cooker are what you need. With a pressure cooker, you can prepare fresh, wholesome ingredients like vegetables, whole grains, beans, and more in the same amount of time it'll take you to pick up a pizza.

An increasing number of cooks across the country are rediscovering what our grandmothers already knew: pressure cookers can make flavorful, nutritious meals in a fraction of the time they take to prepare on the stove. Today's electric pressure cookers are safe, easy to use, and versatile. Many have functions for simmering, browning, and more.

For vegetarians, or those who simply want to reduce the amount of meat they eat in favor of more vegetables and grains, a pressure cooker is a particularly useful tool. With a pressure cooker, you can cook dried beans in less than an hour, while rice and other grains are ready in a fraction of the time that they normally take to cook, even in a rice cooker. With a steamer insert, you can pressure-steam nearly every kind of vegetable to the perfect texture, while locking in nutrients.

In this book, I've made things even easier: Each of these recipes includes no more than five core ingredients (each clearly marked in the ingredient list), supplemented with a handful of staple seasonings, such as oil, salt and pepper, and spices that are likely already in your pantry. This means that you'll be able to shorten your shopping list and prep time, making your time at the supermarket and in the kitchen even more streamlined.

Whether you're new to the world of pressure cookers, or you're looking for new recipes to enjoy with your appliance, I hope *The Five-Ingredient Vegetarian Pressure Cooker Cookbook* will become a trusted resource to help you prepare delicious meals that fit your busy schedule.

Chapter One
THE
BASICS

If you're new to pressure cooking, don't worry. I've got you covered with all the tips and knowledge you'll need to successfully prepare the recipes in this book, and any other pressure cooker recipe you encounter along the way.

You might be surprised to learn that pressure cookers have been around for centuries in one form or another—the first pressure cooker is said to have been invented in the late 1600s by French physicist Denis Papin. Over the years, the models—whether stove top or electric—have evolved, but the idea remains the same: By heating liquid in an enclosed container, pressure builds up and causes the temperature to increase, cooking food faster.

Because pressure cookers are so much more efficient than stove top cooking, they can save energy. They also save water—since evaporation is contained inside the cooker, less water is needed. So, congratulations: Using a pressure cooker is not only saving you time, it's helping reduce your carbon footprint!

Fresh, Fast

In this book you'll find 100 easy-to-prepare recipes; short lists of fresh, nutritious ingredients; and instructions that are easy to understand.

THE CORE FIVE

Each recipe in this book only uses five (or fewer!) main ingredients, which are clearly marked in the ingredient list for each recipe with a small asterisk (✳). In some cases, prepared foods like jarred salsa or prepared pesto will help streamline your shopping list and cut down on your time in the kitchen. What you won't find are heavily processed foods packed with preservatives, sodium, and other unhealthy ingredients.

In addition to the core five ingredients, you'll use basic items that most reasonably stocked kitchens already have on hand. These include:

- Balsamic vinegar
- Rice vinegar
- White wine vinegar
- Butter, unsalted
- Vegetable oil
- Extra-virgin olive oil
- Granulated sugar
- Brown sugar

As for the common spices and seasonings, here's a list of the spices called for in this book:

- Black pepper (I keep a grinder full of whole peppercorns by my stove.)
- Cinnamon, ground
- Cumin, ground
- Dill, dried
- Garlic powder
- Ginger, ground
- Oregano, dried
- Red pepper flakes, crushed
- Salt, kosher
- Salt, bacon (vegetarian)
- Paprika, smoked
- Thyme, dried
- Vanilla extract

ABOUT THIS BOOK

If you looked at the table of contents, you've probably noticed that this book is not organized like the traditional cookbook. I've broken it up instead into three big sections. The first section, Building Blocks, is where you'll find basic recipes and techniques for cooking different types of rice and grains, beans and legumes, and vegetables in your pressure cooker. Some are super-simple, while others are dressed up just enough so you can enjoy them on their own or as a side dish.

The second section, One-Pot Wonders, is the backbone of this book. Here's where you will find easy, flavorful recipes for making breakfasts, main course dinners, soups, and stews. Finally, the Extras section at the end contains fun stuff, such as appetizers, desserts, dips, sauces, and snacks.

A note about cooking times: Each recipe includes a preparation time and a cooking time. This does not include the time it takes for the pressure cooker to come up to pressure. The pressure time can vary depending on the type of pressure cooker, how full it is, and the temperature of the ingredients. You should add 5 to 12 minutes to the cooking time, but you'll get to know your pressure cooker. Also, factor in the time it takes to release the pressure (more on this later). Most recipes call for quick release, which only takes a minute or two, but natural release methods could take 10 to 30 minutes.

BEST BETS

A pressure cooker works especially well for cutting down the cooking time of tough, dense veggies, dried beans, legumes, and grains that typically simmer for a long stretch. You'll be amazed at how quickly you can prepare artichokes, potatoes, beets, and dried chickpeas.

That said, there are some things that don't work well in a pressure cooker. If you're using fresh herbs, for instance, it's best to stir them in after cooking, so their flavors stay bright and their texture is not limp. In many cases, dairy products, too, such as sour cream, cheese, or heavy cream, should be stirred in after cooking or used as a topping, since they can curdle at high heat. The exception is if the food is cooked in a dairy product, like milk or butter.

And finally, many pressure cooker manufacturers caution that some foods should not be cooked in a pressure cooker because they can foam or sputter, which could clog the pressure release valves. These foods include applesauce, cranberries, pearl barley, split peas, noodles, and oatmeal. I've included recipes for oatmeal and applesauce in this book, but I caution against doubling the recipes for this reason.

DRY BEANS IN A PRESSURE COOKER: TO SOAK OR NOT TO SOAK?

One of the biggest advantages of owning one of these appliances is the ability to quickly cook dried beans. Dried beans are usually less expensive and contain less sodium than canned beans, so it's definitely worthwhile to master the cooking techniques in this book.

Opinions are divided on whether or not pressure cooked beans still require the overnight soak recommended for cooking beans on the stove top. There are the three options for pressure cooking dried beans:

Overnight soak: Place the beans in a bowl, cover them with water by several inches, and let them soak for 8 to 12 hours. Before cooking, drain the beans in a colander. The advantages to this extra step is that the beans will cook faster, will stay intact rather than split when they are cooked, and the hard-to-digest enzymes that give some of us intestinal stress are leached away. Be sure to drain the beans well before cooking them according to the recipe method.

Quick soak: If you aren't able to overnight soak, but still want to start your recipe with presoaked beans, opt for this method. Place the beans in a pressure cooker and fill with water to submerge them by about an inch. Lock the lid in place, and set it to cook at high pressure for 6 minutes. Then use the natural pressure release method, drain the beans, and proceed with the recipe. The soaked beans might still split a little, but not as much as if they were being cooked from dry. Always drain the beans before cooking them again per the recipe method.

Dry method: If you don't soak your beans, they'll take a few minutes longer to cook, and the process might cause the beans to split a little. If you're making something like refried beans, this isn't a big deal. Be aware, also, that some people have more trouble digesting beans that are not presoaked and drained.

The bottom line: If time allows, presoaking beans will probably yield the best results. But I've cooked beans without soaking and achieved good results, so don't despair if you find yourself with a sack of dry beans and only half an hour before you need to have a meal on the table! Most of the bean recipes in this book are written for dry beans, but I've tried to give you estimated cooking times if you prefer to soak your beans.

Read, Then Proceed

Different makes of electric pressure cookers work in different ways, so read the instruction manual that comes with your cooker before using it. Most importantly, read about the components to check each time you use the cooker. For instance, it's essential to check the rubber sealing ring for cracks and the various valves, before each use.

UNDERSTANDING THE SETTINGS

Many of today's cookers have multiple settings. The Instant Pot, for instance, has functions for steam, slow cook, brown (or sauté), pressure cook, porridge, poultry, and more. The recipes in this book only use pressure cook and brown functions.

Many electric pressure cookers have high and low pressure levels, and sometimes even medium. Typically, high pressure is 9 to 11 pounds per square inch (psi), while low pressure is 4 to 6 psi. Instruction manuals should include the psi range that corresponds to the high and low settings. Keep in mind that electric pressure cookers maintain a lower psi level than a stove top pressure cooker (which usually cooks at 13 to 15 psi). The recipes in this book are written especially for electric pressure cookers, so if you attempt any of these recipes using a stove top pressure cooker, you will want to reduce the cooking time by a couple of minutes.

The brown function on a pressure cooker is handy for sautéing or browning ingredients before pressure cooking. Sautéing onions or other aromatics in a little oil or butter softens and caramelizes them, making for a better flavor and texture. Starting with hot ingredients also will shorten the amount of time it takes for the pot to come up to pressure.

THE RIGHT RELEASE

An electric pressure cooker is designed with safety features that will keep the lid locked into place until the pressure inside has been released completely. Don't *ever* try to force the lid open. There are two ways to release pressure in an electric pressure cooker safely.

Quick release: This method typically takes a couple of minutes. When the food is done pressure cooking, most pressure cookers automatically switch to a keep warm setting. You can leave it on this setting or turn it off, then release the pressure manually by turning the steam vent (check the instruction manual to learn how to do this on your machine). Be sure that you do this carefully, standing back and using tongs or an oven mitt, as turning the valve will cause a geyser of hot steam. When the steam no longer escapes, it is safe to open the lid.

Natural release: This method is a lot slower than the quick-release method. When the food is finished cooking, let the pressure release on its own without turning the valve. You can do this with the cooker still on the keep warm setting (handy if your cooker has a "count up" so you can monitor the amount of time it's taking to release pressure), or you can turn it off or unplug it so that the contents cool faster. Usually there is a visible float valve that indicates the contents are under pressure—when this drops down, it means that pressure has been released and the lid will unlock. It's a good idea to turn the steam release valve before doing so, just to make sure the pressure has been completely released. Natural release could take as long as 15 to 30 minutes, depending on the contents in the cooker. If you get impatient after 10 to 15 minutes, releasing the remaining pressure by turning the release valve will not affect the end result of your finished dish.

When to use which method? Most of the recipes in this book call for the quick-release method, since this is best for ensuring that the contents aren't over-cooked. However, if you are cooking ingredients that are likely to foam, like oatmeal, beans, pasta, or soup, the natural-release method is best.

Safety first: When you open your pressure cooker lid, make sure to open it away from your face, as hot steam will probably still rise out of the pot when it opens. Also beware of condensation that will drop off the lid, which will also be piping hot and can burn you if it drips on your skin.

CLEANING AND CARE

Keeping your pressure cooker clean and in good repair ensures that you can use it safely and effectively for years to come. Your instruction manual will offer specifics on which parts can be removed for cleaning. But in general, you can take these steps after each use:

1. Unplug the power cord.
2. Remove the inner pot and wash it inside and out with hot water and dish detergent. Some inner pots are even dishwasher safe. Let the pot air dry or wipe it dry with a clean dishtowel.
3. Using a wet sponge or dishrag, clean the inside and outside of the lid and rinse it with clean water. Take care to clean the sealing ring (this can usually be removed for more thorough cleaning) and any other removable parts as indicated in your manual.
4. Use a damp paper towel to wipe the exterior clean and to wipe up crumbs and food residue along the inner rim.
5. If your unit has a condensation collector, empty it and rinse it out.

Using Your Pressure Cooker: Dos and Don'ts

The way a pressure cooker works is fairly simple: Food and liquid are sealed inside of a vessel, then the heating element heats the contents until steam builds up. The very hot steam causes the temperature inside of the pot to increase significantly more than it would in a traditional pot. This increased temperature—up to 250°F—penetrates the food and cooks it more quickly, as much as 70 percent faster than on the stove. The rubber ring inside the lid prevents steam from escaping, while several valves regulate the pressure. Finally, a locking mechanism on the handle prevents the cooker from being opened until the interior pressure is completely released.

These tips will help you prepare the recipes in this book, and any pressure cooker recipes, safely and successfully.

DOS

Do read the instructions for your pressure cooker before using it. If you have misplaced your manual, many manufacturers make them available online, or you can call the company's toll-free customer service number to request a new one.

Do check the gasket and valves each time before use. If the rubber ring is brittle, or has any signs of wear and tear, it needs to be replaced. Manufacturers sell replacement gaskets; it's a good idea to invest in an extra one to keep on hand just in case yours gets damaged.

Do dry the outside of the inner pot before putting it in the unit. Wiping drips of food or water from the outside of the pot will help keep the inside of the appliance clean. This prevents damage to the heating element as well.

Do read the whole recipe before you begin cooking. This way, you can make sure you have all the ingredients called for, the tools you need to prep the ingredients, and enough time to make it.

Do feel free to experiment. I hope the simple recipes in this book will encourage you to get to know the wonderful technique of pressure cooking and will help you adapt these recipes to your own personal preferences.

DON'TS

Don't force the pressure cooker open. Pressure cookers are designed to remain locked until all the steam pressure has escaped and it's safe to open. If your cooker won't open, make sure to manually release every last bit of pressure.

Don't overfill the pressure cooker pot. Most manufacturers recommend that you fill the inside pot no more than two-thirds full. If you're cooking something that expands, like rice, you should fill it no more than halfway.

Don't forget to make sure the pressure release valve is turned toward the closed position. If you used the quick-release method the last time you used the cooker, chances are it's still in that position. Make sure it's closed so that the steam will build inside the cooker.

Don't double the recipe. These recipes, as well as most pressure cooker recipes, are tested for the appropriate cooking time and to safely fill a 6-quart cooker. If you double the recipe, you might risk overfilling the cooker and the cooking time might be different. It's better to cook the food in two batches.

Don't fear the pressure cooker. Many people balk at the concept of pressure cooking, recalling tales they've heard of exploding cookers. Today's cookers have multiple safety features in place. As long as you follow the instructions, there's no risk of the cooker exploding and spewing chili all over your ceiling!

Prep, Perfected

Taking time to prep your ingredients properly and making sure all the equipment you need is on hand ensures you stay organized in the kitchen.

KNIFE SKILLS

Herbs and vegetables should be cut to the specific size and shape directed in the recipe to make sure they cook properly. Here are some of the knife cuts that you will see in the recipes in this book. While it's not essential for each piece to be a perfect cube or slice, it is important for them to be roughly the same size. Not only does this make for a nicer presentation, but it also ensures that everything is cooked evenly so you don't end up with some pieces that are underdone, while others that are mushy and overcooked.

- **Minced:** chopped as finely as possible. This is typically used for herbs, garlic, fresh ginger, shallots, and other flavoring ingredients.
- **Diced:** cut into cubes. The size will be indicated in the recipe. Fine dice means pieces of less than ¼ inch, while medium dice is ½ inch, and large dice is ¾ to 1 inch.
- **Julienne:** cut into narrow strips. The easiest way to do this is to cut a vegetable into slices first, then cut each slice into strips of the same width as the slices are thick.

KITCHEN SETUP

Here are some tools that are handy to have at the ready:

- **Trash bowl:** Keep a bowl for vegetable trimmings, eggshells, produce stickers, and other trash next to your cutting board. If you compost, make sure to separate out trash from compostable matter.
- **Wooden spoon or silicone spatula:** A heat-resistant tool can be used to stir ingredients and scrape down the sides of your cooking spot. If your pressure cooker pot has a nonstick interior, be sure to use a nonmetal tool that won't scratch the coating.
- **Kitchen tongs:** A set of medium-length tongs is useful for removing food from the interior pot, lifting out ramekins, or turning the pressure release valve.
- **Silicone oven mitt:** The steam coming out of your pot will be even hotter than steam coming off a pot of boiling water. A silicone oven mitt will protect hands better than cloth ones. Even better, buy a pair so you can safely lift the inner pot out of your appliance.

BULK COOKING AND SHOPPING

Since many of the ingredients in these recipes overlap, consider buying basics, such as beans and rice, in bulk to save money. You can also become a more efficient cook if you plan your menu ahead of time and even prep ingredients on the weekend so they'll be ready to cook on busy weeknights. Some things you can do ahead of time:

- Dice onions, carrots, and celery and keep them, separated, in zip-top freezer bags in the refrigerator.
- Mince herbs and mix them with a little bit of extra-virgin olive oil. Portion them and freeze them in mini ice cubes or dolloped onto wax paper.
- Grate cheese and store it in a zip-top bag in the refrigerator.

STORE-BOUGHT TIME-SAVERS

Buying pre-prepped ingredients saves time. What's more, jarred or frozen versions will keep better and longer than fresh. Look for peeled and chopped garlic and ginger in a jar or frozen; tubes of puréed fresh herbs; freeze-dried herbs that can sub for fresh versions; and fresh or frozen diced onions or celery. Bags of prewashed greens are also time-savers.

I'm also a big fan of liquid stock or broth concentrates that are mixed with hot water. These taste just as good as the cans or cartons of stock, but are more efficient to buy since they are in a small jar or bottle that can be kept in the refrigerator, as opposed to a large container of ready-to-use stock that needs to be used up or frozen within a week.

SUPER EASY STORAGE

Many of these recipes freeze beautifully, especially soups and stews. If you have left-overs, portion them into freezer-safe, zip-top bags or glass or plastic containers with airtight lids and freeze them. Be sure to label them with the contents, quantity, and the date. In most cases, you can defrost the meal overnight in the refrigerator and then heat on the stove or in the microwave.

COOK TIMES CHEAT SHEET

The following charts are a great guide for cooking some of the most basic ingredients you'll find in this book. Keep in mind that the times are for when the appliance has reached pressure, which requires additional time.

Rice

All use high pressure. For white rice varieties, use 1 cup rice to 1½ cups liquid. For brown rice, use 1 cup rice to 1¼ cups liquid. Add a teaspoon of oil or butter to the pot to reduce foaming.

RICE	COOK TIME	RELEASE METHOD AND TIME
WHITE LONG-GRAIN RICE	3 minutes	10 minutes natural release, then quick release
WHITE SHORT-GRAIN RICE	8 minutes	7 minutes natural release, then quick release
BROWN RICE	20 minutes	10 minutes natural release, then quick release
BASMATI RICE	3 minutes	10 minutes natural release, then quick release
JASMINE RICE	2 minutes	10 minutes natural release, then quick release

Beans

All use high pressure and natural-release method.

BEAN (1 CUP)	COOK TIME, SOAKED	COOK TIME, DRY
BLACK BEANS	4 to 6 minutes	28 to 32 minutes
PINTO BEANS	8 to 10 minutes	23 to 25 minutes
CANNELLINI BEANS	8 to 10 minutes	28 to 30 minutes
RED KIDNEY BEANS	8 to 10 minutes	23 to 25 minutes
LENTILS	NA	10 to 12 minutes
CHICKPEAS	12 to 14 minutes	40 minutes

Other Grains

All use high pressure.

GRAIN	GRAIN-TO-LIQUID RATIO	COOK TIME	RELEASE METHOD AND TIME
FARRO	1 cup farro to 2½ cups liquid	10 minutes	quick release
QUINOA	1 cup quinoa to 1½ cups liquid	2 minutes	10 minutes natural release
ROLLED OATS	⅓ cup oats to ⅔ cup liquid	10 minutes	natural release
STEEL-CUT OATS	¼ cup oats to ¾ cup liquid	15 minutes	natural release

Eggs (in shell)

All methods use low pressure and quick-release method.

DONENESS	COOK TIME
SOFT-COOKED	3 minutes
MEDIUM-COOKED	4 minutes
HARD-COOKED	5 minutes

Vegetables

All methods use high pressure and the quick-release method unless otherwise indicated. It's better to undercook vegetables than overcook them. If the vegetables are undercooked when you check, replace the lid and let them steam for a few more minutes. Unless otherwise indicated, all vegetables should be peeled if necessary and cut into large chunks or pieces.

VEGETABLE	COOK TIME
ARTICHOKES (WHOLE)	5 to 11 minutes, depending on size
ASPARAGUS (WHOLE)	1 minute
BEETS	11 to 13 minutes
BROCCOLI	2 to 3 minutes
CARROTS	3 to 5 minutes

CAULIFLOWER	2 to 3 minutes
CORN (WHOLE EARS ON RACK)	2 minutes
GREEN BEANS	1 minute at low pressure
GREENS	4 to 6 minutes
SWEET POTATOES	5 to 6 minutes
SQUASH, ACORN (HALVED)	6 to 8 minutes
SQUASH, BUTTERNUT	5 to 7 minutes
WHITE POTATOES	5 to 7 minutes
ZUCCHINI OR YELLOW SQUASH	1 to 3 minutes

Chapter Two
BUILDING BLOCKS

GRAINS
25

BEANS
39

VEGETABLES
51

GRAINS

26	Basic White Rice
27	Basic Brown Rice
28	Brown Rice with Scallions
29	Creamy Coconut Rice
30	Herby Brown Rice Pilaf
31	Farro with Mushrooms and Walnuts
32	Basic Quinoa
33	Quinoa, Tabbouleh Style
34	Quinoa with Pine Nuts and Parmesan
35	Cheese Grits
36	Classic Polenta
37	Barley Bowl with Kale and Carrots

Basic White Rice

PREP TIME: 5 MINUTES • COOK TIME: 3 MINUTES AT HIGH PRESSURE, NATURAL RELEASE

SERVES 4 Making white rice in a matter of minutes is certainly one of the biggest advantages to owning an electric pressure cooker. With a little tweaking of the rice-to-water ratio and the cooking time, I've found the best formula for making fluffy, perfectly cooked white rice. While rinsing the rice before cooking is not essential, doing so rinses some of the starch away, resulting in fluffier, more distinct grains of rice.

GLUTEN-FREE

SOY-FREE

NUT-FREE

VEGAN

1 cup long-grain white rice
1 cup water
¼ teaspoon kosher salt

1. In the pot of the pressure cooker or in a fine-mesh strainer, rinse the rice several times until the water seems less chalky. Drain well.

2. Add the rice, water, and salt to the pressure cooker. Stir to combine and scrape down any loose grains of rice into the liquid.

3. Lock on the lid and set the timer for 3 minutes at high pressure. When the timer goes off, natural release for 10 minutes, then quick release any remaining pressure. Remove the lid and stir the rice with a fork to fluff. If any water remains, cover the cooker and let the rice sit for 5 minutes until the water is absorbed.

Cooking Tip *This recipe can be doubled using the same cooking time and 1-to-1 ratio of rice and water. Just be aware that it will take longer for the cooker to come up to pressure, and make sure not to overfill your pressure cooker. Rice, since it expands, should only fill the pressure cooker no more than halfway.*

Basic Brown Rice

PREP TIME: 5 MINUTES • COOK TIME: 20 MINUTES AT HIGH PRESSURE, NATURAL RELEASE

SERVES 4 Unlike white rice, brown rice has not had its bran and germ layers removed, which is where all the nutrients are stored. In my opinion, it's also where all the flavor and texture are, too. Swapping brown rice for white will give you a boost of fiber, vitamin B, manganese, iron, and essential fatty acids, among other nutrients. It takes a bit longer to cook, but I think the chewy, nutty flavor and the dietary benefits make it well worth the effort.

GLUTEN-FREE
SOY-FREE
NUT-FREE
VEGAN

* 1 cup long-grain brown rice
1¼ cups water
¼ teaspoon kosher salt

1. In the pot of the pressure cooker or in a fine-mesh strainer, rinse the rice several times until the water seems less chalky. Drain well.

2. Add the rice, water, and salt to the pressure cooker. Stir to combine and scrape down any loose grains of rice into the liquid.

3. Lock on the lid and set the timer for 20 minutes at high pressure. When the timer goes off, natural release for 10 minutes, then quick release any remaining pressure. Remove the lid and stir the rice with a fork to fluff. If any water remains, cover the cooker and let the rice sit for 5 minutes until the water is absorbed.

Brown Rice with Scallions

PREP TIME: 5 MINUTES • COOK TIME: 25 MINUTES AT HIGH PRESSURE, NATURAL RELEASE

SERVES 4 Asian flavors dress up this brown rice, making it delicious as a side dish on its own, or a flavorful base for the Thai Green Curry (page 93) or a stir-fry. For variations, add some frozen edamame to the rice after cooking (let it steam with the lid on until the edamame is heated through), or garnish it with a sprinkling of black or white sesame seeds or seaweed seasoning, a condiment you can find in Asian supermarkets.

NUT-FREE
VEGAN

1 tablespoon vegetable oil

❋ 1 teaspoon sesame oil

❋ 2 scallions, thinly sliced, white and green parts separated

❋ 1 cup short-grain brown rice

❋ 1 cup low-sodium vegetable stock or broth

1 cup water

❋ 2 tablespoons low-sodium soy sauce

1. With the pressure cooker on the brown or sauté setting, heat the vegetable oil and sesame oil in the pot. Add the white parts of the scallion and sauté, stirring frequently, for about 3 minutes, until softened and fragrant.

2. Stir in the brown rice and toast it for about 1 minute until the rice grains are coated with the oil. Add the vegetable stock, water, and soy sauce. Stir to combine, scraping any grains of rice down the sides of the pot.

3. Lock on the lid and set the timer for 25 minutes at high pressure. When the timer goes off, turn off the pressure cooker and let the pressure natural release for 10 minutes. Quick release any remaining pressure and open the cooker. If the rice is not fully cooked or if liquid remains, cover the cooker and let the rice sit and steam for 5 minutes more.

4. Fluff the rice with a fork, transfer to a serving bowl, and garnish it with the green slices of scallion.

Ingredient Tip *To change this recipe up, try substituting ponzu sauce for the soy sauce and top with fresh chopped cilantro instead of the remaining scallions. The citrusy flavor of the ponzu sauce adds a nice tanginess to the rice.*

Creamy Coconut Rice

PREP TIME: 5 MINUTES • COOK TIME: 3 MINUTES AT HIGH PRESSURE, NATURAL RELEASE

SERVES 4 This slightly sweet rice is a favorite of my mother-in-law, who serves it on its own as a side dish or as a base for stir-fried veggies. Cooked in coconut milk, this rice has a creamy consistency and a lightly sweet flavor. I like to stir a handful of frozen edamame beans into the rice after it's finished cooking and let them steam for a few minutes until they're hot, which makes it a more substantial side dish.

GLUTEN-FREE

SOY-FREE

NUT-FREE

VEGAN

✳ 1½ cups jasmine rice

✳ 1 (15-ounce) can
    coconut milk

½ cup water

1 teaspoon granulated sugar

¼ teaspoon kosher salt

Ingredient Tip *Other kinds of white rice, such as sushi rice and other short-grained rice, work well in this recipe.*

1. Rinse the rice in a colander or in the pot of your pressure cooker, draining it well.

2. Place the rice in the pressure cooker pot and add the coconut milk, water, sugar, and salt. Stir to combine, scraping down grains of rice from the side of the pot.

3. Lock on the lid and set the timer for 3 minutes at high pressure. When the timer goes off, turn off the cooker and natural release for 7 minutes, then quick release any remaining pressure. Open the cooker and stir the rice with a fork before serving.

Herby Brown Rice Pilaf

PREP TIME: 10 MINUTES • COOK TIME: 22 MINUTES AT HIGH PRESSURE, NATURAL RELEASE

SERVES 4 This fresh-tasting side dish is a versatile and easy recipe to pair with just about any entrée. Try different kinds of herbs, such as dill, tarragon, basil, or even mint. It's nice with mushroom stock or vegetarian chicken-flavored stock, too. Other ways of mixing up the flavors include starting with minced garlic, leeks, or shallots instead of onion, or topping with toasted nuts or Parmesan cheese just before serving.

1. With the pressure cooker on the sauté or brown setting, heat the olive oil. Add the onion and sauté, stirring frequently, until the onion is softened and translucent, about 5 minutes.

2. Add the rice, and stir for about 30 seconds until toasted a bit. Add the vegetable stock and stir to combine, scraping down any stray rice grains or onion from the side of the pot.

3. Lock on the lid and set the timer for 22 minutes at high pressure. When the timer goes off, natural release the pressure for 10 minutes, then quick release any remaining pressure. Open the lid and use a fork to fluff the rice. If some liquid remains, leave the lid on for 5 minutes until it is absorbed.

4. Stir in the parsley and thyme. Add the salt and pepper. Serve hot.

GLUTEN-FREE

SOY-FREE

NUT-FREE

VEGAN

1 tablespoon extra-virgin olive oil

✳ 1 small white onion, minced

✳ 1 cup long-grain brown rice

✳ 1¼ cups vegetable stock

✳ 1 tablespoon minced fresh parsley

✳ 1 teaspoon minced fresh thyme

⅛ teaspoon kosher salt

⅛ teaspoon freshly ground black pepper

Ingredient Tip *If you only have dry herbs, use about half as much: 1½ teaspoons of dried parsley and ½ teaspoon dried thyme. You can add the dried herbs with the broth so that they can infuse their flavor into the rice while it cooks.*

Farro with Mushrooms and Walnuts

PREP TIME: 10 MINUTES ● COOK TIME: 10 MINUTES AT HIGH PRESSURE, QUICK RELEASE

SERVES 4 If you have never tried farro, you're in for a treat. It's an ancient strain of wheat from Italy, with a pleasingly nutty flavor and a chewy, toothsome texture. Look for semi-pearled farro, which has some of the bran removed and cooks faster. If you can only find whole farro, it should be soaked overnight before cooking, and it will take about twice as long to cook in the pressure cooker.

SOY-FREE
VEGAN

1 tablespoon extra-virgin olive oil
✳ 1 shallot, minced
✳ 2 cups (about 4 ounces) assorted sliced mushrooms
✳ 1 cup farro
✳ 2½ cups mushroom stock
¼ teaspoon kosher salt
⅛ teaspoon freshly ground black pepper
✳ ½ cup roughly chopped toasted walnuts

1. With the pressure cooker on the sauté or brown setting, heat the olive oil. Add the shallot and sauté, stirring frequently, until the shallot is softened and translucent, about 5 minutes.

2. Add the mushrooms and cook, stirring occasionally, until they soften, 4 to 5 minutes. Add the farro and stir for about 30 seconds in the oil mixture, until toasted a bit. Add the mushroom stock and stir to combine, scraping down any stray bits from the side of the pot.

3. Lock on the lid and set the timer for 10 minutes at high pressure. When the timer goes off, quick release the pressure and remove the lid. Season the farro with the salt and pepper, and toss with the walnuts. Serve hot or warm.

Basic Quinoa

PREP TIME: 2 MINUTES • COOK TIME: 3 MINUTES AT HIGH PRESSURE, NATURAL RELEASE

SERVES 4 Quinoa is just about the perfect food for a vegetarian or vegan. It's one of the few complete protein plant products, containing all of the essential amino acids. It has a mild, grassy flavor and is a good alternative to rice for pilaf-type side dishes. Or you can chill it and make it into a salad for a potluck. Store-bought packaged quinoa usually does not need to be rinsed, unless instructed to do so on the package directions.

GLUTEN-FREE
SOY-FREE
NUT-FREE
VEGAN

* 1 cup white quinoa
1¾ cups water
⅛ teaspoon kosher salt

Cooking Tip *You can also find red and black quinoa varieties at the market. These take a little longer to cook. If you are using red, black, or a tricolor quinoa mix, cook for 5 minutes at high pressure.*

1. Place the quinoa, water, and salt in the pressure cooker pot.

2. Lock on the lid and set the timer for 3 minutes at high pressure. When the timer goes off, natural release the pressure for 5 minutes. Quick release any remaining pressure and remove the lid. If water remains, cover the cooker and let sit for 5 minutes until the water is absorbed.

3. Fluff the quinoa with a fork. Serve hot. Or, to serve as a chilled salad, spread the cooked quinoa on a large plate or baking sheet to cool before using.

Quinoa, Tabbouleh Style

PREP TIME: 15 MINUTES • COOK TIME: 3 MINUTES AT HIGH PRESSURE, NATURAL RELEASE

SERVES 4 This simple grain makes the ideal base for a not-quite-traditional tabbouleh salad. Fresh tomatoes and parsley brighten this satisfying side dish.

GLUTEN-FREE

SOY-FREE

NUT-FREE

VEGAN

1. Place the quinoa, water, and ⅛ teaspoon of salt in the pressure cooker pot. Lock on the lid and set the timer for 3 minutes at high pressure. When the timer goes off, natural release the pressure for 5 minutes. Quick release any remaining pressure and remove the lid. If water remains, cover the cooker and let the quinoa sit for 5 minutes for any additional water to absorb.

2. Fluff the quinoa with a fork. Spread the quinoa on a baking sheet or a large plate to cool.

3. When the quinoa has cooled, transfer it to a bowl and toss it with the onion powder, parsley, mint, and tomatoes. Drizzle the lemon juice and olive oil over the salad and toss to combine. Add the remaining 1 teaspoon of salt and the pepper. Serve at room temperature. This salad can be made up to 1 day ahead of time.

* 1 cup white quinoa
  1¾ cups water
  1⅛ teaspoons kosher
  salt, divided
  ½ teaspoon onion powder
* 1 cup chopped fresh parsley
* ½ cup chopped fresh mint
* 4 plum tomatoes, seeded
  and chopped
* 3 tablespoons freshly
  squeezed lemon juice
  2 tablespoons extra-virgin
  olive oil
  ⅛ teaspoon freshly ground
  black pepper

Preparation Tip *To remove the seeds and pulp from the tomatoes, quarter them lengthwise. Working over a sink, use your clean finger to dig out the pulp and seeds from the inside of the tomatoes, rinsing them away under cool running water.*

Quinoa with Pine Nuts and Parmesan

PREP TIME: 10 MINUTES • COOK TIME: 3 MINUTES AT HIGH PRESSURE, NATURAL RELEASE

SERVES 4 This pilaf-style dish is my take on one of my favorite packaged side dish mixes. Pine nuts can be a bit pricey, but they're used sparingly here. If you prefer, you can use sliced or slivered almonds. Red quinoa can be used instead of white; just cook it for 5 minutes at high pressure.

GLUTEN-FREE
SOY-FREE

1 tablespoon extra-virgin olive oil
* 1 small yellow onion, minced
* 1 cup white quinoa
* 1¾ cups vegetable broth
* ¼ cup finely grated Parmesan cheese
* ¼ cup toasted pine nuts
⅛ teaspoon kosher salt
⅛ teaspoon freshly ground black pepper

Preparation Tip *To toast nuts, heat them in a dry skillet over medium-high heat for 4 to 5 minutes, shaking the pan frequently or stirring them so they toast evenly on all sides.*

1. With the pressure cooker on the sauté or brown setting, heat the olive oil until it shimmers. Add the onion and sauté, stirring frequently, until it is soft and begins to brown, 6 to 7 minutes. Stir in the quinoa and vegetable broth.

2. Lock on the lid and set the timer for 3 minutes at high pressure. When the timer goes off, natural release the pressure for 5 minutes. Quick release any remaining pressure and remove the lid. If any liquid remains, cover the cooker and let the quinoa sit for 5 minutes to allow the quinoa to absorb the remaining liquid. Fluff the quinoa with a fork.

3. Sprinkle the Parmesan cheese and pine nuts over the quinoa and use the fork to lightly mix it in. Add the salt and pepper. Serve hot.

Cheese Grits

PREP TIME: 10 MINUTES • COOK TIME: 10 MINUTES AT HIGH PRESSURE, NATURAL RELEASE

SERVES 4 Grits are a mainstay in the South, where I live. They're a staple side dish alongside scrambled eggs for breakfast or as part of a main course for dinner. They're the American version of polenta, but are made from a white-kernel variety of corn. You can find specialty grits from small mills, like Anson Mills or Bob's Red Mill, at specialty stores or online. They're worth seeking out for their more pronounced flavor and texture.

1. With the pressure cooker on the sauté or brown setting, heat 1 tablespoon of butter until it melts, using a wooden spoon to spread it to coat the bottom of the pot. Add the water and 1 teaspoon of salt. Sprinkle the grits into the water and stir with a whisk to combine.

2. Lock on the lid and set the timer for 10 minutes at high pressure. When the timer goes off, natural release the pressure for 10 minutes. Quick release any remaining pressure and remove the lid.

3. Stir the grits with a whisk to break up any lumps. Stir in the remaining 2 tablespoons of butter, the cream, and the cheese. Add the remaining ⅛ teaspoon of salt and the pepper. Serve hot.

GLUTEN-FREE
SOY-FREE
NUT-FREE

3 tablespoons unsalted butter, divided

3½ cups water

1⅛ teaspoons kosher salt, divided

☀ 1 cup coarse grits

☀ 2 tablespoons heavy (whipping) cream

☀ 1 cup (about 3 ounces) grated sharp Cheddar cheese

⅛ teaspoon freshly ground black pepper

Ingredient Tip *Try different types of cheese in grits, such as Gouda, goat cheese, or pepper Jack cheese.*

Classic Polenta

PREP TIME: 5 MINUTES • COOK TIME: 8 MINUTES AT HIGH PRESSURE, NATURAL RELEASE

SERVES 4 Polenta, with its silky texture and creamy flavor, is a ubiquitous Northern Italian dish. And why not? It's a perfect starting point for a delicious meal. Try it topped with Spicy Kale (page 56) or Hearty Tomato Sauce (page 137) and a generous handful of shredded mozzarella cheese. A mound of sautéed mushrooms or roasted eggplant are also good toppings. Be sure to buy regular polenta, not the instant variety, which won't give you the same results.

GLUTEN-FREE
SOY-FREE
NUT-FREE

4 cups water

1 tablespoon extra-virgin olive oil

☀ 1 cup polenta

2 tablespoons unsalted butter

☀ ½ cup finely grated Parmesan cheese

⅛ teaspoon kosher salt

⅛ teaspoon freshly ground black pepper

1. With the pressure cooker on the sauté or brown setting, heat the water and olive oil until they are steaming. Sprinkle in the polenta and stir to combine.

2. Lock on the lid and set the timer for 8 minutes at high pressure. When the timer goes off, turn off or unplug the pressure cooker and natural release the pressure for 10 minutes. Quick release any remaining pressure and remove the lid.

3. Stir in the butter and Parmesan cheese, and add the salt and pepper. Serve hot.

Serving Tip *I like to use this recipe to make polenta cakes. Pour the cooked polenta onto a baking sheet until it's set, and slice it or cut it into rounds with a biscuit cutter. Then, fry them in a little bit of oil to make cakes. They're great served under a bed of sautéed greens or with a spoonful of marinara sauce ladled over them.*

Barley Bowl with Kale and Carrots

PREP TIME: 15 MINUTES • COOK TIME: 17 MINUTES AT HIGH PRESSURE, NATURAL RELEASE

SERVES 4 The chewy texture of barley makes it a good base for this hearty bowl dinner, which includes kale and carrots, and is dressed with a maple vinaigrette and shaved Parmesan cheese. Dinosaur kale (also known as lacinto or Tuscan kale) comes in long, spear-like stems with wrinkled, dark-green leaves. Its slightly bitter flavor contrasts nicely with the sweet dressing. For a variation, try the recipe with diced butternut squash and shredded Brussels sprouts instead of carrots and kale.

1. Place the barley in the pressure cooker pot and add the water and vegetable oil. Stir to combine, scraping down any stray barley grains from the side of the pot.

2. Lock on the lid and set the timer for 16 minutes at high pressure.

3. Meanwhile, in a small bowl, whisk together the vinegar, maple syrup, dry mustard, salt, and pepper. While continuing to whisk, drizzle in the olive oil until the dressing is emulsified. Set aside.

4. When the timer goes off, natural release the pressure for 10 minutes. Quick release any remaining pressure and remove the lid. Give the barley a stir, then layer the kale leaves on top of the barley. Place the carrots on top of the kale, without stirring the vegetables into the barley.

5. Lock on the lid and set the timer for 1 minute at high pressure. When the timer goes off, quick release the pressure and remove the lid. Strain any remaining liquid from the barley and vegetables in a colander and transfer the barley mixture to a serving dish.

6. Whisk the dressing to re-emulsify, if needed, then drizzle it over the barley mixture. Toss to combine, then stir in the grated Parmesan cheese. Serve warm garnished with several Parmesan curls.

GLUTEN-FREE

SOY-FREE

NUT-FREE

* 1 cup pearled barley
  4 cups water
  1 tablespoon vegetable oil
  ¼ cup apple cider vinegar
* 1 tablespoon maple syrup
  ¼ teaspoon dry mustard
  ¼ teaspoon kosher salt
  ⅛ teaspoon freshly ground black pepper
  ¼ cup extra-virgin olive oil
* 2 cups dinosaur kale, stemmed and leaves chopped
* 4 carrots, peeled and diced
* ¼ cup grated Parmesan cheese, plus several curls for garnish

Serving Tip *To make Parmesan curls, drag a vegetable peeler slowly along the edge of a block of Parmesan cheese. Garnish each bowl with a lemon wedge, if desired.*

BEANS

40   Basic Black Beans

41   Basic Pinto Beans

42   Basic Chickpeas

43   Indian-Style Lentils

44   Cuban-Style Black Beans

45   Rosemary White Beans

46   Two-Bean Salad

47   Refried Beans

48   Barbecue Beans

49   Butter Beans with Tomatoes and Carrots

Basic Black Beans

PREP TIME: 10 MINUTES • COOK TIME: 35 MINUTES AT HIGH PRESSURE, NATURAL RELEASE

MAKES ABOUT 7 CUPS These beans are great to have on hand to add to a salad, tuck into a tortilla, add to a soup, or top with a fried egg. Bacon salt mimics the unctuous flavor of a smoked ham hock or real bacon, but if you can't find it at your supermarket or specialty food store, you can use a combination of kosher salt and smoked paprika or chipotle seasoning.

GLUTEN-FREE

SOY-FREE

NUT-FREE

VEGAN

1 tablespoon vegetable oil

1 medium onion, diced

2 garlic cloves, minced

1 pound dried black beans, rinsed

1 bay leaf

2 teaspoons bacon salt

½ teaspoon kosher salt

1. With the pressure cooker on the sauté or brown setting, heat the vegetable oil. Add the onion and sauté, stirring frequently, until the onion is softened and translucent, about 5 minutes. Add the garlic and sauté for 30 seconds, stirring constantly. Add the beans and enough water to cover them by about 2 inches (without exceeding the maximum fill level of your pressure cooker). Add the bay leaf.

2. Lock on the lid and set the timer for 35 minutes at high pressure. When the timer goes off, natural release the pressure.

3. Remove and discard the bay leaf. Stir in the bacon salt and the kosher salt. Beans will keep in an airtight container in the refrigerator for up to a week, or frozen for up to 6 months.

Cooking Tip *You can soak black beans overnight if you want to cut down on the cooking time, but don't worry if you forget—their skins aren't as likely to split as softer-textured beans. If you presoak your beans, they will only take 6 minutes at high pressure to cook, with a natural release.*

Basic Pinto Beans

PREP TIME: 10 MINUTES • COOK TIME: 10 MINUTES AT HIGH PRESSURE, NATURAL RELEASE

MAKES ABOUT 6 CUPS These beans are flavorful enough to enjoy on their own, but also can serve as a foundation for any recipe calling for canned beans, whether it's chili, a burrito, bean dip, and more. I personally like a bowl of it topped with some avocado slices and crumbled queso fresco. The best place to buy dried beans is from a super-market or natural food store that has bulk bins, as they're more likely to be fresh.

GLUTEN-FREE

SOY-FREE

NUT-FREE

VEGAN

- 1 pound dried pinto beans, soaked overnight, drained
- 2 garlic cloves, minced
- ½ yellow onion, diced
- 1 teaspoon ground cumin
- ½ teaspoon smoked paprika
- 1 bay leaf
- 1 tablespoon vegetable oil
- 1 teaspoon kosher salt

1. Place the soaked beans in the pot of a pressure cooker. Add the garlic and onion, and enough water to cover the beans by about 1 inch (but make sure that the pot is not more than halfway full or exceeding the maximum level specified by your user manual). Stir in the cumin, paprika, bay leaf, and oil.

2. Lock on the lid and set the timer for 10 minutes at high pressure. When the timer goes off, natural release the pressure. Remove and discard the bay leaf and add the salt. These beans will keep in an airtight container in the refrigerator for up to a week, or frozen for up to 6 months.

Ingredient Tip *Soaking the beans beforehand will speed up the cooking time and will help keep the beans from splitting out of their skins, but I've had good success putting dried beans right in the pressure cooker. If you do it this way, they'll need 25 to 30 minutes at high pres-sure, and another 2 cups of water (make sure the water covers the beans by about an inch, as much of it will be absorbed).*

Basic Chickpeas

PREP TIME: 2 MINUTES • COOK TIME: 45 MINUTES AT HIGH PRESSURE, NATURAL RELEASE

MAKES ABOUT 6 CUPS Chickpeas, which are also called garbanzo beans, are a good source of fiber, protein, and essential amino acids. Plus, they're an important part of numerous cuisines, including Mediterranean, Middle Eastern, and Indian. Use them in stews and soups, in a salad, or to make hummus, the popular Middle Eastern dip. The cooked chickpeas can also be roasted with your preferred spice blend for a delicious snack or to add to salads.

1. Place the chickpeas in the pressure cooker pot and pour in enough water to cover them by about 2 inches (about 8 cups of water). Stir in the salt.

2. Lock on the lid and set the timer for 45 minutes at high pressure. When the timer goes off, natural release the pressure for 10 minutes. Quick release any remaining pressure and remove the lid. Drain the chickpeas in a colander and use as desired.

GLUTEN-FREE

SOY-FREE

NUT-FREE

VEGAN

* 1 pound dry chickpeas, rinsed
½ teaspoon kosher salt

Preparation Tip *If you soak the chickpeas overnight or for at least 10 hours, you can cook them at high pressure for 15 minutes, using the same amount of water and salt. Natural release as directed in step 2.*

Indian-Style Lentils

PREP TIME: 10 MINUTES • COOK TIME: 4 MINUTES AT HIGH PRESSURE, QUICK RELEASE

SERVES 4 Pressure cookers are a fixture in many Indian kitchens, probably because they do such a great job at making such iconic dishes in a short amount of time. This lentil stew is my take on Indian dal. Make sure to use red lentils instead of brown or green ones. The red variety break down during cooking, which gives this dish its creamy consistency. Serve it with a dollop of plain yogurt on top and with some warm naan bread or pita to scoop up the lentils.

GLUTEN-FREE

SOY-FREE

NUT-FREE

VEGAN

2 teaspoons extra-virgin olive oil

❋ ⅓ cup diced yellow onions

3 cups water

❋ 1 cup red lentils, rinsed

1 bay leaf

½ teaspoon garlic powder

1 teaspoon ground cumin

❋ 1 teaspoon Indian curry powder

❋ ½ teaspoon ground turmeric

¼ teaspoon ground cayenne pepper

½ teaspoon kosher salt

1. With the pressure cooker at the brown or sauté setting, heat the olive oil. Add the onion and sauté, stirring frequently, about 5 minutes or until it is translucent. Add the water, lentils, bay leaf, and garlic powder; stir to combine.

2. Lock on the lid and set the timer for 4 minutes at high pressure.

3. While the lentils are cooking, in a small bowl combine the cumin, curry powder, turmeric, cayenne, and salt. Set aside.

4. When the timer goes off, quick release the pressure. Remove the lid, and stir the spice blend into the lentils. Switch the pressure cooker to the brown or sauté setting and continue to cook the lentils, stirring frequently, for about 5 minutes, to allow the flavors to meld. Serve hot.

Cuban-Style Black Beans

PREP TIME: 15 MINUTES • COOK TIME: 35 MINUTES AT HIGH PRESSURE, NATURAL RELEASE

SERVES 6 TO 8 Onion, green peppers, and garlic form the flavorful base for this black bean recipe, which is my take on a ubiquitous—and so delicious—Cuban dish. Serve it ladled over Basic White Rice (page 26) or Basic Brown Rice (page 27); it's equally delicious on Cheese Grits (page 35). If you start with dried black beans that have been soaked overnight, the cooking time will only be 6 minutes at high pressure.

GLUTEN-FREE

SOY-FREE

NUT-FREE

VEGAN

1 tablespoon vegetable oil

❋ 1 medium onion, diced

❋ 2 green bell peppers, diced

❋ 4 garlic cloves, minced

❋ 1 pound dried black beans, rinsed

1 bay leaf

1 teaspoon dried oregano

1 teaspoon ground cumin

1 teaspoon smoked paprika

2 tablespoons apple cider vinegar

1 tablespoon granulated sugar

1 teaspoon kosher salt

1. With the pressure cooker on the sauté or brown setting, heat the vegetable oil. Add the onion and bell peppers and sauté, stirring frequently, until the onion is softened and translucent, about 5 minutes. Add the garlic and sauté for 30 seconds, stirring constantly. Add the beans to the pot and enough water to cover them by about 2 inches, without exceeding the maximum fill level of your pressure cooker. Add the bay leaf, oregano, cumin, paprika, and vinegar.

2. Lock on the lid and set the timer for 35 minutes at high pressure. When the timer goes off, natural release the pressure. Remove and discard the bay leaf.

3. Spoon about 1 cup of beans into a medium bowl. Mash them with the back of a spoon until they form a chunky purée. Stir them back into the beans in the pot. Stir in the sugar and salt.

Rosemary White Beans

PREP TIME: 10 MINUTES • COOK TIME: 25 MINUTES AT HIGH PRESSURE, NATURAL RELEASE

SERVES 4 In my opinion, rosemary is an underrated herb. Its pungent, bright flavor goes great with the creamy, earthy flavor of Cannellini beans. For the olive oil that's drizzled onto the beans at the end, I like to use a really flavorful, peppery oil that really stands out. Serve this recipe alongside sautéed greens, with some crusty bread, or double the recipe to bring to a potluck. It's a great side dish that goes with just about everything.

GLUTEN-FREE
SOY-FREE
NUT-FREE
VEGAN

- 8 ounces dried Cannellini beans, rinsed
- 2 garlic cloves, minced
  1 bay leaf
  3 tablespoons extra-virgin olive oil, divided
- 2 plum tomatoes, seeded and chopped
- 1 tablespoon minced fresh rosemary
  ⅛ teaspoon kosher salt
  ⅛ teaspoon freshly ground black pepper

1. In the pot of a pressure cooker, add the beans and fill it with enough water to cover the beans by about 2 inches. Add the garlic, bay leaf, and 1 tablespoon of olive oil, and stir to combine.

2. Lock on the lid and set the timer for 25 minutes at high pressure. When the timer goes off, natural release the pressure for 10 minutes. Quick release any remaining pressure and remove the lid. If the beans aren't tender, lock the lid back on and cook for an additional 3 to 5 minutes at high pressure. Drain the beans in a colander, discarding the bay leaf. Transfer the beans to a serving bowl.

3. Toss the beans with the tomatoes, rosemary, salt, pepper, and the remaining 2 tablespoons of olive oil. Serve hot.

Two-Bean Salad

PREP TIME: 10 MINUTES • COOK TIME: 24 MINUTES AT HIGH PRESSURE, NATURAL RELEASE

SERVES 6 TO 8 Dried black beans and kidney beans take the same amount of time to cook, so you can combine them for this recipe. I've kept the ingredients simple here, but if you want to jazz up this salad, try adding diced red bell pepper for color, crumbled queso fresco, or diced avocado. It's a fun summer salad to serve at a picnic, and it's great folded inside a warm tortilla.

1. Place the kidney beans and black beans in the pressure cooker pot and add enough water to cover the beans by about 2 inches. Stir in 1 tablespoon of olive oil.

2. Lock on the lid and set the timer for 24 minutes at high pressure. When the timer goes off, natural release for 10 minutes. Quick release any remaining pressure. Drain the beans in a colander and rinse them under cool water.

3. Place the beans in a large bowl and add the corn and cilantro.

4. In a small bowl, whisk together the lime juice, remaining 2 tablespoons of olive oil, salt, and pepper. Drizzle the dressing over the bean mixture, stirring gently to combine. This salad can be made a day ahead and refrigerated in a covered container until ready to serve.

GLUTEN-FREE
SOY-FREE
NUT-FREE
VEGAN

* 6 ounces dried kidney beans, rinsed
* 6 ounces dried black beans, rinsed
* 3 tablespoons extra-virgin olive oil, divided
* 1 (1-pound) bag frozen corn kernels, thawed
* ¼ cup chopped fresh cilantro
* Juice of 1 lime
* 1 teaspoon kosher salt
* ¼ teaspoon freshly ground black pepper

Ingredient Tip *You can soak these beans overnight or for 8 to 10 hours. Drain them and cook them on high pressure for 6 minutes with natural release, as instructed in step 2.*

Refried Beans

PREP TIME: 5 MINUTES • COOK TIME: 35 MINUTES AT HIGH PRESSURE, NATURAL RELEASE

SERVES 6 TO 8 Whip up a batch of these refried beans. They're so much better-tasting—and better for you—than the sodium-laden canned variety. Enjoy them as a base for bean dip, rolled up in a burrito, or layered with corn tortillas and a fried egg on top. If you are a fan of spicy food, stir in a few generous dashes of your favorite hot sauce as you're mashing the beans.

GLUTEN-FREE
SOY-FREE
NUT-FREE
VEGAN

1 tablespoon vegetable oil, plus more if needed

½ medium yellow onion, diced

2 garlic cloves, crushed

1 pound dried pinto beans, rinsed

5 cups water

1 tablespoon ground cumin

1 teaspoon chipotle seasoning

2 teaspoons kosher salt

1. With the pressure cooker on the sauté or brown setting, heat the vegetable oil. Add the onion and sauté, stirring frequently, until the onion is softened and translucent, about 5 minutes. Add the garlic and sauté for 30 seconds, stirring constantly. Add the beans and the water. The water should cover the beans by about 1 inch; add more if needed. Stir in the cumin and chipotle seasoning.

2. Lock on the lid and set the timer for 35 minutes at high pressure. When the timer goes off, turn off or unplug the pressure cooker and natural release the pressure.

3. Use a wooden spoon or a potato masher to mash the beans, or use an immersion blender for a smoother texture. If the beans seem dry and pasty, add an additional tablespoon of vegetable oil and a little water until they have a creamy consistency. Stir in the salt. Refried beans will keep in the refrigerator for 3 to 4 days in an airtight container, or can be frozen in a freezer bag or a freezer-safe container for up to 2 months.

Barbecue Beans

PREP TIME: 15 MINUTES • COOK TIME: 30 MINUTES AT HIGH PRESSURE, QUICK RELEASE

SERVES 8 Your favorite barbecue sauce, along with a few other ingredients, is the perfect shortcut to homemade baked beans. I like a sauce that is not super-spicy, but is heavy on the molasses, brown sugar, and smoky flavor. If you want to ramp up the smokiness, try stirring in a teaspoon of smoked paprika, bacon salt, or chipotle seasoning. Great northern beans, which are larger, can also be used to make this version of baked beans.

NUT-FREE
VEGAN

❋ 1 pound dried navy beans, rinsed

8 cups water, plus more if needed

2 tablespoons vegetable oil, divided

❋ 1 medium yellow onion, diced

❋ 2 cups barbecue sauce

¼ cup brown sugar

¼ cup apple cider vinegar

1. In the pressure cooker pot, place the beans, water, and 1 tablespoon of vegetable oil. The water should cover the beans by at least 2 inches.

2. Lock on the lid and set the timer for 25 minutes at high pressure. When the timer goes off, quick release the pressure. Open the lid and stir the beans. They should be just a little underdone. Drain the beans in a colander, and set aside.

3. Wipe out the interior of the pressure cooker. With the setting on brown or sauté, heat the remaining 1 tablespoon of vegetable oil until it shimmers. Add the onion and sauté, stirring frequently, until the onion is translucent and softened, about 5 minutes. Return the beans to the pressure cooker, and add the barbecue sauce, brown sugar, and vinegar. Stir to combine.

4. Lock on the lid and set the timer for 5 minutes at high pressure. When the timer goes off, quick release the pressure. Open the lid and stir the beans well before serving.

Butter Beans with Tomatoes and Carrots

PREP TIME: 10 MINUTES • COOK TIME: 17 MINUTES AT HIGH PRESSURE, QUICK RELEASE

SERVES 4 TO 6 I wasn't a fan of butter beans when I was a kid, but maybe if I'd had them prepared this way, with a savory, tomato-studded broth, I would have been. Also known as lima beans, butter beans are most certainly named for their creamy, buttery flavor. Rancho Gordo, the specialty bean producer, sells them on their website along with a beautiful speckled version called Christmas lima beans. Garnish the finished dish with a sprinkle of fresh oregano or baby basil for some extra flavor.

GLUTEN-FREE
SOY-FREE
NUT-FREE
VEGAN

1 tablespoon extra-virgin olive oil

❋ 1 small yellow onion, diced

❋ 8 ounces dried lima beans, rinsed

1 bay leaf

❋ 1 (15-ounce) can diced tomatoes, undrained

❋ 2 cups vegetable broth

❋ 4 carrots, peeled and diced into ¾-inch pieces

1 teaspoon dried thyme

⅛ teaspoon kosher salt

⅛ teaspoon freshly ground black pepper

Ingredient Tip *Dried butter beans or lima beans aren't very common, so if you have trouble finding them, you can use white beans instead and increase the cooking time to 25 minutes at high pressure.*

1. With the pressure cooker on the brown or sauté setting, heat the oil until it shimmers. Add the onion and sauté, stirring frequently, until the onion is softened and translucent, about 5 minutes. Add the lima beans, bay leaf, and enough water (about 4 cups) to cover the beans by about 2 inches.

2. Lock on the lid and set the timer for 14 minutes at high pressure. When the timer goes off, quick release the pressure. The beans should be mostly cooked but still a bit firm.

3. Drain the beans in a colander and return the beans and bay leaf to the pressure cooker pot. Add the tomatoes, broth, carrots, thyme, salt, and pepper.

4. Lock on the lid and set the timer for 3 minutes at high pressure. When the timer goes off, quick release the pressure and remove the lid. Remove and discard the bay leaf and give the beans a stir. Serve hot.

VEGETABLES

52 Steamed Broccoli or Cauliflower, Four Ways

53 Steamed Artichokes

54 Steamed Asparagus, Four Ways

55 Seasoned Bok Choy

56 Spicy Kale

57 Stewed Collard Greens

58 Green Beans, Four Ways

59 Maple-Glazed Carrots

60 Beets, Two Ways

62 Spaghetti Squash with Cheddar Cheese

63 Sweet Potatoes with Ginger and Cilantro

64 New Potato Salad

65 Smoky Mashed Potatoes

66 Braised Red Cabbage

67 Corn on the Cob, Four Ways

68 Cider-Braised Brussels Sprouts

69 Vegetable Stock

Steamed Broccoli or Cauliflower, Four Ways

PREP TIME: 10 MINUTES • COOK TIME: 2 MINUTES AT HIGH PRESSURE, QUICK RELEASE

SERVES 4 Perfectly steamed broccoli, or its fellow crucifer cauliflower, lends itself to plenty of variations. I've outlined four here to inspire you. They're also delicious drizzled with a little olive oil and seasoned lightly with salt and pepper. Try to cut the pieces into as uniformly sized as possible, so they all cook at the same rate. This is a good way to prepare the vegetables to use in a recipe that calls for cooked or frozen broccoli or cauliflower.

SOY-FREE
NUT-FREE

1 cup water
✳ 1 broccoli head, cut into bite-size florets (about 4 cups)
or
✳ 1 cauliflower head, cut into bite-size florets (about 4 cups)

1. Place a steamer insert in the pot of a pressure cooker. Add the water to the pot. Place the broccoli or cauliflower in the insert.

2. Lock on the lid and set the timer for 2 minutes at high pressure. When the timer goes off, quick release the pressure and open the lid. Use tongs to transfer the broccoli or cauliflower to a serving dish.

3. Top or toss broccoli with one of the following:

- 2 tablespoons melted unsalted butter and ¼ cup toasted bread crumbs that has been mixed with 2 tablespoons grated Parmesan cheese. Season with salt and pepper.
- 1 tablespoon extra-virgin olive oil and ¼ cup crumbled feta or goat cheese. Season with salt and pepper.
- 1 tablespoon extra-virgin olive oil. Sprinkle with red pepper flakes, salt, and pepper.
- 2 tablespoons prepared or homemade balsamic vinaigrette

Steamed Artichokes

PREP TIME: 10 MINUTES • COOK TIME: 15 MINUTES AT HIGH PRESSURE, QUICK RELEASE

SERVES 4 Artichokes were the first thing I made in my pressure cooker. They're one of my favorite foods, but not one I make often because of the time involved trimming the leaves and steaming the artichokes. Cutting the spikes off is still a labor of love, but at least the pressure cooker greatly reduces the cooking time. I love artichoke leaves dipped in melted butter mixed with a squeeze of lemon. Mayonnaise, aioli, or vinaigrette are other popular dips.

GLUTEN-FREE

SOY-FREE

NUT-FREE

VEGAN

* 4 medium artichokes
* 1 lemon, halved
  1 cup water

Ingredient Tip *Some people believe that the sign of a ripe artichoke is not how it looks, but how it sounds: an artichoke should squeak a little when it's squeezed. The leaves should be tightly packed, and the artichoke should feel heavy.*

1. To prepare the artichokes, use kitchen shears to trim the spiky tips off all the artichoke leaves. Pull off any tough leaves off the very bottom and use a paring knife to trim off the stem. Rub the cut parts of the artichoke with the lemon to avoid discoloring.

2. Place a steamer insert or a rack in the pressure cooker pot. Add the water to the pot. Arrange the artichokes in the pressure cooker, stacking them if necessary.

3. Lock on the lid and set the timer for 15 minutes at high pressure. When the timer goes off, quick release the pressure, open the lid, and remove the artichokes with tongs. Serve hot or cool or use in another recipe.

Steamed Asparagus, Four Ways

PREP TIME: 5 MINUTES • COOK TIME: 1 MINUTE AT HIGH PRESSURE, QUICK RELEASE

SERVES 4 Asparagus is one of the first vegetables to come into season in the spring. The elegant stalks can be pencil-thin or as thick around as a thumb; the thinner versions are more tender, so choose those if you can. For thicker stalks, some people like to use a vegetable peeler to shave off a bit of the stalk to make it more tender. You also might need to cook thicker stalks for an additional minute when cooking at high pressure.

GLUTEN-FREE
SOY-FREE

½ cup water
✳ 1 pound asparagus, trimmed

Ingredient Tip To trim asparagus, grasp a stalk between the middle and bottom part. Gently bend until it snaps, probably about an inch from the bottom, and discard the snapped-off end. Snap each spear in the same way or, to save time, line up the rest of the stalks on your cutting board and cut them all to the same length.

1. Place a steamer insert in the pot of a pressure cooker. Add the water to the pot. Place the asparagus in the insert. If the stalks are too long, it's fine to lean them against the sides of the cooker.

2. Lock on the lid and set the timer for 1 minute at high pressure. When the timer goes off, quick release the pressure and open the lid. Use tongs to transfer the asparagus to a serving dish.

3. Top or toss asparagus with one of the following:

-   2 tablespoons melted unsalted butter mixed with ½ teaspoon freshly grated lemon zest
-   2 tablespoons champagne vinaigrette and 1 tablespoon slivered almonds
-   ¼ cup hollandaise sauce
-   1 tablespoon hazelnut oil and 1 tablespoon chopped hazelnuts. Season with salt and pepper.

Seasoned Bok Choy

PREP TIME: 5 MINUTES • COOK TIME: 1 MINUTE AT HIGH PRESSURE, QUICK RELEASE

SERVES 4 Bok choy is like two veggies rolled into one: flavorful leafy greens and the crisp stalks. I prefer the baby version, which are super tender and perfectly, naturally portioned for a serving. This makes a great vegetable side dish to any main course. Or you can turn this into a meal by serving it atop brown rice with edamame or sautéed tofu.

NUT-FREE

VEGAN

1 cup water

4 baby bok choy heads, quartered lengthwise

1 tablespoon rice wine vinegar

1 teaspoon sesame oil

1 tablespoon toasted sesame seeds

1. Place a steamer insert in the pot of a pressure cooker. Add the water to the cooker and mound the bok choy in the steamer.

2. Lock on the lid and set the timer for 1 minute at high pressure. When the timer goes off, quick release the pressure and remove the lid. Use a tongs to transfer the bok choy to a serving platter or bowl.

3. In a small bowl, whisk together the vinegar and sesame oil. Drizzle it over the bok choy. Sprinkle the sesame seeds over the bok choy and serve immediately.

Spicy Kale

PREP TIME: 1 MINUTE • COOK TIME: 5 MINUTES AT HIGH PRESSURE, QUICK RELEASE

SERVES 4 Kale is ideal for the pressure cooker, which tenderizes its sturdy leaves. This version livens it up with a tangy splash of vinegar and a sprinkling of red pepper flakes. It's great on its own, or try chopping the kale more finely before you cook it and toss with cooked pasta.

GLUTEN-FREE
SOY-FREE
NUT-FREE
VEGAN

1 tablespoon extra-virgin olive oil

✺ 2 garlic cloves, minced

✺ 1 kale bunch, stemmed and chopped or 1 (1-pound) bag chopped kale

1½ cups water

1 tablespoon red wine vinegar

½ teaspoon red pepper flakes

¼ teaspoon kosher salt

1. With the pressure cooker on the sauté or brown setting, heat the olive oil. Add the garlic and sauté for 30 seconds, stirring constantly. Add the kale and water to the pressure cooker.

2. Lock on the lid and set the timer for 5 minutes at high pressure. When the timer goes off, quick release the pressure, remove the lid, and toss the cooked greens with the vinegar, red pepper flakes, and salt. Serve hot.

Stewed Collard Greens

PREP TIME: 10 MINUTES • COOK TIME: 20 MINUTES AT HIGH PRESSURE, NATURAL RELEASE

SERVES 4 Collard greens are in the kitchen of every respectable meat-and-three restaurant in the South. While they've simmered for hours at these establishments, you can get the same tender result in the pressure cooker in a fraction of the time. In the South, they're typically cooked with ham hocks or bacon to give them a smoky, meaty flavor. Smoked paprika is a good substitute for the meat, imbuing the greens with a similarly smoky flavor.

1. With the pressure cooker on the sauté or brown setting, heat the vegetable oil until it shimmers. Add the onion and sauté, stirring frequently, until it is softened and translucent, about 5 minutes. Add the collard greens, vegetable broth, and paprika.

2. Lock on the lid and set the timer for 20 minutes at high pressure. When the timer goes off, natural release for 10 minutes. Quick release any remaining pressure and remove the lid

3. Stir in the vinegar, hot sauce, salt, and pepper. Serve hot.

GLUTEN-FREE

SOY-FREE

NUT-FREE

VEGAN

1 tablespoon vegetable oil

* 1 yellow onion, diced
* 1 collard greens bunch, roughly chopped
* 2 cups vegetable broth

1 teaspoon smoked paprika

1 tablespoon cider vinegar

* ½ teaspoon hot sauce

⅛ teaspoon kosher salt

⅛ teaspoon freshly ground black pepper

Preparation Tip *To prepare the collard greens, rinse the leaves well by immersing them in a sink full of cool water. Fold the leaves in half along the stem and use a chef's knife to cut away the toughest part of the stem. Then stack a few leaves at a time, roll them up into a cigar shape, and slice into wide ribbons. You can further chop the ribbons if desired.*

Green Beans, Four Ways

PREP TIME: 10 MINUTES • COOK TIME: 2 MINUTES AT HIGH PRESSURE, QUICK RELEASE

SERVES 4 Steamed in the pressure cooker, these beans are so easy to make that it gives you the chance to get creative with how you season them. Check out my four options, or get creative with flavor combinations of your own. This is a great way to prepare fresh green beans when they're at their peak in late summer, but you can use frozen beans for this recipe if fresh aren't available; just add a minute to the cooking time when cooking at high pressure.

1. Add the water to the pressure cooker pot. Place a steamer insert in the cooker. Place the beans in the steamer insert.

2. Lock on the lid and set the timer for 2 minutes at high pressure. When the timer goes off, quick release the pressure and open the lid. Use tongs to transfer the beans to a serving bowl.

3. Season the beans with one of the following:

- Toss beans with salt, pepper, 2 teaspoons extra-virgin olive oil, and 2 tablespoons finely grated Parmesan cheese.
- Place 1 tablespoon of unsalted butter on the hot beans and add salt and pepper. Toss with tongs to melt the butter and coat the beans. Sprinkle with ¼ cup toasted slivered almonds.
- Drizzle 2 teaspoons sesame oil over the beans and add salt and pepper. Toss the beans with tongs to coat them with the oil. Sprinkle 1 tablespoon toasted sesame seeds over the beans.
- Sauté 1 cup mixed sliced mushrooms in butter until softened, 6 to 7 minutes. Stir the mushrooms into the beans and add salt and pepper. Top with ¼ cup packaged fried onions.

GLUTEN-FREE

1 cup water

* 4 pounds green beans, trimmed

Preparation Tip *To prepare green beans, break or trim the ends off each bean. You can do this by lining up a handful of beans on the cutting board and using a sharp knife to cut off all the ends at once.*

Maple-Glazed Carrots

PREP TIME: 8 MINUTES • COOK TIME: 2 MINUTES AT HIGH PRESSURE, QUICK RELEASE

SERVES 4 My kids are always thrilled when this sweet side dish makes an appearance on the dinner table. It's not surprising—these tender carrots are coated in a maple sauce, enticing even the staunchest vegetable hater. Bagged baby carrots are convenient to use for this recipe, but if you want a more sophisticated presentation, use a bunch of small carrots from the farmers' market. Prepare them whole, but peeled, perhaps with a little bit of the greens still attached.

1. Place the water and carrots in the pot of a pressure cooker.

2. Lock on the lid and set the timer for 2 minutes at high pressure. When the timer goes off, quick release the pressure, open the cooker, and switch to the brown setting.

3. Add the butter, maple syrup, salt, and pepper. Sauté the carrots for 2 to 3 minutes, or until most of the remaining liquid evaporates. Sprinkle with the fresh thyme. Serve hot or warm.

GLUTEN-FREE
SOY-FREE
NUT-FREE

1 cup water
* 1 pound baby carrots
1½ tablespoons unsalted butter
* 1½ tablespoons pure maple syrup
¼ teaspoon kosher salt
Pinch freshly ground black pepper
* 1 teaspoon fresh minced thyme

Ingredient Tip *Be sure to spring for pure maple syrup, rather than the artificial breakfast syrup. Real maple syrup is thinner and not quite as cloyingly sweet.*

Beets, Two Ways

PREP TIME: 10 MINUTES • COOK TIME: 12 TO 16 MINUTES AT HIGH PRESSURE, QUICK RELEASE

SERVES 4 There are those who love beets and will order them any time they see them on a menu—myself included. I think anyone who says they don't like beets just hasn't had them prepared well. Once you make beets in the pressure cooker, you won't want them any other way. They are tender, juicy, and have a vibrant ruby hue. I've given you a couple of serving options, or simply use this method as a starting point for your own favorite preparation.

1. Place a steamer insert or a rack in the pot of a pressure cooker. Add the water to the cooker. Place the beets on the steamer insert.

2. Lock on the lid and set the timer for 13 minutes at high pressure, less if the beets are very small. When the timer goes off, quick release the pressure and open the lid. Test the beets by piercing them with a fork; the fork should easily pierce the beets, which should still be firm but with a bit of give and feel a little soft when squeezed. If they still seem very hard, like an uncooked potato, lock the lid back on and cook at high pressure for 3 more minutes.

3. When the beets are done, remove them from the cooker with tongs and let them rest until cool enough to handle, slip the skins from the beets, they should come right off. Quarter the beets and slice into bite-size pieces.

GLUTEN-FREE
SOY-FREE
NUT-FREE

1 cup water
* 1 pound medium-size beets, root and stems trimmed

FOR VERSION 1
2 tablespoons unsalted butter
2 tablespoons granulated sugar
2 tablespoons apple cider vinegar
⅛ teaspoon kosher salt
Pinch freshly ground black pepper

FOR VERSION 2
2 tablespoons unsalted butter
⅛ teaspoon kosher salt
Pinch freshly ground black pepper
* ¼ cup finely grated Parmesan cheese
* 1 tablespoon minced fresh parsley

4. **To prepare version 1,** remove the rack and pour the water out of the pressure cooker. With the setting on sauté or brown, melt the butter. Add the sugar and vinegar and stir until the sugar dissolves. Add the beets, and stir to coat them evenly with the vinegar mixture. Add the salt and pepper. Serve hot or warm. (Note: If you want to serve this recipe chilled, replace the butter with extra-virgin olive oil; otherwise, the butter will congeal.)

5. **To prepare version 2,** place the hot sliced beets into a bowl and toss with the butter, salt, and pepper until the butter is melted and coats the beets. Add the Parmesan and parsley and toss to distribute.

Ingredient Tip *If your beets came with their greens still attached, don't throw them away! They are wonderful roughly chopped and quickly sautéed in extra-virgin olive oil and garlic, just as you would enjoy spinach.*

Spaghetti Squash with Cheddar Cheese

PREP TIME: 5 MINUTES • COOK TIME: 7 MINUTES AT HIGH PRESSURE, QUICK RELEASE

SERVES 2 Spaghetti squash is so unusual—once cooked, the flesh separates into strands like its namesake pasta. It has a very neutral flavor, unlike its sweeter squash relatives, which makes it really versatile. Because the cheese is really the star of this dish, seek out a really sharp, good-quality aged cheddar. This simple dish makes for a quick side dish or, paired with a simple salad, a delicious lunch.

GLUTEN-FREE
SOY-FREE
NUT-FREE

❋ 1 spaghetti squash (about 3 pounds)
1 cup water
1 tablespoon unsalted butter
❋ ½ cup (about ½ ounce) shredded aged Cheddar cheese
Pinch kosher salt
Pinch freshly ground black pepper

1. Slice the stem end off the spaghetti squash and halve it lengthwise. Use a spoon to scoop out the seeds and the pulp. Place a rack or a steamer insert in the pressure cooker pot, add the water to the pot. Place the squash on the rack or steamer, cut-side down. If the squash halves don't fit, they can be set in the pot at an angle or overlapping each other.

2. Lock on the lid and set the timer for 7 minutes at high pressure. When the timer goes off, quick release the pressure, open the cooker, and remove the squash with tongs.

3. When the squash is cool enough to handle, divide the butter between each squash half. Use a fork to scrape the flesh of the squash into spaghetti-like strands, while mixing the butter in as it melts. The outer part of the squash serves as a bowl. Sprinkle the cheese over the squash, and stir it into the squash. Add the salt and pepper, and serve hot or warm.

Sweet Potatoes with Ginger and Cilantro

PREP TIME: 10 MINUTES • COOK TIME: 9 MINUTES AT HIGH PRESSURE, QUICK RELEASE

SERVES 4 Growing up, I always enjoyed sweet potatoes mixed with butter and brown sugar. It's only been recently that I've realized how beautifully this tuber pairs with other flavors, even unexpected ones. This recipe is delicious served atop Creamy Coconut Rice (page 29), or alongside a veggie stir-fry. If you want to get really adventurous, seek out purple sweet potatoes, which have vivid purple flesh and an intensely rich flavor. They're also denser than regular sweet potatoes, so they might require an extra minute or two of cooking when cooked at high pressure.

1. Place a rack or a steamer insert in the pressure cooker pot and add the water to the pot. Place the potatoes on the rack or steamer and sprinkle the grated ginger over them.

2. Lock on the lid and set the timer for 9 minutes at high pressure. When the timer goes off, quick release the pressure, open the cooker, and remove the potatoes with tongs or a slotted spoon, transferring them to a serving bowl.

3. Sprinkle the potatoes with the brown sugar and sesame oil. Cover the bowl with aluminum foil for about 5 minutes to allow the sugar to melt. Just before serving, remove the foil and add the salt and pepper. Gently stir the potatoes to coat them with the sugar syrup, then add the cilantro.

GLUTEN-FREE
SOY-FREE
NUT-FREE
VEGAN

1 cup water

4 medium sweet potatoes (about 2 pounds), peeled and cut into 1½-inch chunks

1 tablespoon grated fresh ginger

2 tablespoons brown sugar

1 teaspoon sesame oil

½ teaspoon kosher salt

¼ teaspoon freshly ground black pepper

¼ cup minced fresh cilantro

Cooking Tip *To grate fresh ginger, use the edge of a spoon to scrape off the skin, then use a rasp-style grater, like a Microplane, to grate the knob of ginger into pulp. Even easier is to buy a jar of minced ginger, which keeps for several months in the refrigerator. You can find it in the Asian section of a well-stocked supermarket.*

New Potato Salad

PREP TIME: 15 MINUTES • COOK TIME: 4 MINUTES AT HIGH PRESSURE, QUICK RELEASE

SERVES 8 Potato salad is a summertime favorite, and this version is a must-have menu item for your next barbecue. Be sure to cut the potatoes to a uniform size so they'll all have the same consistency. The cut pieces should be a large bite size, a little bigger than an inch. Because mayonnaise is the star of this recipe, it's definitely worthwhile to seek out a high-quality, flavorful brand. I am a fan of the regional brand Duke's.

GLUTEN-FREE
NUT-FREE

1 cup water
* 2 pounds new potatoes, washed and halved
* ¾ cup mayonnaise
  2 tablespoons red wine vinegar
* 1 tablespoon whole grain mustard
  2 teaspoons dried dill
  1 teaspoon kosher salt
  ⅛ teaspoon freshly ground black pepper
* 2 celery stalks, diced
* ¼ cup minced red onion

1. Place a rack or steamer insert in the pressure cooker pot and add the water to the pot. Place the potatoes in the insert.

2. Lock on the lid and set the timer for 4 minutes at high pressure. When the timer goes off, quick release the pressure. Remove the potatoes (they should still be firm but can be pierced with a fork) and let them cool completely.

3. In a small bowl, whisk together the mayonnaise, vinegar, mustard, dill, salt, and pepper until smooth.

4. Place the cooled potatoes in a large mixing or serving bowl and add the celery and onion. Spoon the mayonnaise mixture over the potatoes and gently toss to distribute the dressing. Chill for 1 hour or more, and serve cold. This potato salad can be made a day ahead and stored, covered, in the refrigerator until ready to serve.

Smoky Mashed Potatoes

PREP TIME: 15 MINUTES • COOK TIME: 10 MINUTES AT HIGH PRESSURE, QUICK RELEASE

SERVES 4 TO 6 Russet potatoes are best for mashing because they have a high starch content and less moisture. They are easily identifiable by their brown, matte-looking exterior. Yukon gold potatoes, which have waxy, yellow-looking skin, can also be used in this recipe. You'll get slightly denser potatoes, but they'll be no less delicious. Cooking the potatoes elevated on the rack keeps them fluffy, while cooking them submerged in water can result in soggy, heavy potatoes.

1. Place a rack or a steamer insert in the pressure cooker pot, add the water to the pot. Place the potatoes on the rack or steamer.

2. Lock on the lid and set the timer for 10 minutes at high pressure. When the timer goes off, quick release the pressure and open the cooker. Transfer the potatoes, with a slotted spoon, to a colander set in the sink. Remove the rack from the pressure cooker, pour out the water, and return the drained potatoes to the pressure cooker pot.

3. Add the butter and the milk and use a potato masher or a wooden spoon to mash the potatoes until they are mostly smooth, with a few chunks remaining. Add the paprika, salt, and pepper, and stir to combine. Add more salt and pepper if needed. If the potatoes cool off too much, turn on the keep warm or the sauté setting to heat them back up, stirring constantly. Serve warm.

GLUTEN-FREE
SOY-FREE
NUT-FREE

1 cup water

✻ 4 large russet potatoes, peeled, rinsed, and quartered

⅓ cup unsalted butter

✻ ¾ cup whole milk

1 teaspoon smoked paprika

½ teaspoon kosher salt

¼ teaspoon freshly ground black pepper

Cooking Tip *If you want silky-smooth, restaurant-quality potatoes, use a potato ricer before adding the butter and milk. Pressing the chunks of cooked potato through a ricer purées them into a super-smooth texture with no chunks. After all the potatoes have been riced, stir in the butter, milk, and seasonings.*

Braised Red Cabbage

PREP TIME: 10 MINUTES • COOK TIME: 8 MINUTES AT HIGH PRESSURE, QUICK RELEASE

SERVES 6 This red cabbage dish is earthy, tangy, and sweet all at once. It's remarkably versatile: Serve it hot or warm as a side dish, or pass it around at a potluck chilled or at room temperature. It's a good substitute for sauerkraut; try it with veggie sausages or atop buttered noodles or German spaetzle. It's destined to become a family favorite.

1. With the pressure cooker on the sauté or brown setting, heat the butter until it melts. Add the onion and sauté, stirring frequently, until the onion is softened and translucent, about 5 minutes. Add the broth, vinegar, brown sugar, celery seeds, salt, and black pepper. Stir to combine.

2. Thinly slice the cabbage and add it to the pot. Use tongs or a spoon to toss the cabbage with the broth mixture.

3. Lock on the lid and set the timer for 8 minutes at high pressure. When the timer goes off, quick release the pressure, remove the lid, and stir the cabbage.

GLUTEN-FREE
SOY-FREE
NUT-FREE

2 tablespoons
   unsalted butter

* 1 small yellow onion,
   thinly sliced

* 1 cup vegetable broth
   ¼ cup red wine vinegar
   2 tablespoons brown sugar

* 1 tablespoon celery seeds
   ½ teaspoon kosher salt,
   plus more if needed
   ¼ teaspoon freshly ground
   black pepper, plus more
   if needed

* 1 (2 to 2½ pounds)
   red cabbage head

Preparation Tip *To easily core and slice the cabbage, cut the head into quarters. Then use the knife at an angle to cut out the white core. Slice the wedges thinly with a chef's knife or a mandoline slicer.*

Corn on the Cob, Four Ways

PREP TIME: 10 MINUTES • COOK TIME: 2 MINUTES AT HIGH PRESSURE, NATURAL RELEASE

SERVES 4 Ask five foodies the best way to prepare corn on the cob and you'll get five different answers. I'd like to offer up my own method, which is quick and easy and keeps the kernels tender and juicy. Because I could eat fresh corn on the cob just about every day in the summer, I've come up with a few variations on how to enjoy it. Try these, but certainly come up with your own versions—the sky's the limit!

GLUTEN-FREE

SOY-FREE

NUT-FREE

1 cup water

✳ 4 fresh corn ears, husked and cut or broken in half

1. Place a steamer insert or a rack in the pot of a pressure cooker. Add the water to the cooker and pile the corn on the insert.

2. Lock on the lid and set the timer for 2 minutes at high pressure. When the timer goes off, natural release the pressure. Open the lid and remove the corn with tongs.

3. While the corn is hot, top the ears with one of the following combinations:

- Brush each ear with coconut oil, squeeze a wedge of lime over each cob, and sprinkle with bacon salt.
- Slather the ears with mayonnaise and sprinkle with crumbled Cojita cheese and chili powder.
- Make a compound butter by stirring 1 tablespoon minced fresh basil and a pinch salt into 2 tablespoons very soft unsalted butter. Spread the butter on the hot corn.
- Slather each ear with unsalted butter. Sprinkle with garlic salt and squeeze a wedge of fresh lemon over each cob.

Cider-Braised Brussels Sprouts

PREP TIME: 12 MINUTES • COOK TIME: 4 MINUTES AT HIGH PRESSURE, QUICK RELEASE

SERVES 4 Brussels sprouts are a staple on my Thanksgiving table. This recipe is particularly nice on turkey day or for any fall meal when this crucifer is at its peak. Apple cider offsets the mild bitter flavor of the sprouts, while mustard adds a piquant touch to the mixture. To prepare the sprouts, trim off a thin sliver of the stem, and cut them in half, stem to end.

1. With the pressure cooker on the brown or sauté setting, heat the oil until it shimmers. Add the shallot and sauté, stirring frequently, until it is softened and translucent, 4 to 5 minutes. Add the apple cider and mustard. Stir to combine. Add the Brussels sprouts and stir to coat with the cider.

2. Lock on the lid and set the timer for 4 minutes at high pressure. When the timer goes off, quick release the pressure and remove the lid. Sprinkle the Brussels sprouts with the thyme, salt, and pepper. Remove with a slotted spoon and serve hot.

GLUTEN-FREE

SOY-FREE

NUT-FREE

VEGAN

1 tablespoon extra-virgin olive oil

* 1 shallot, diced

* 1 cup apple cider

* 1 teaspoon Dijon mustard

* 1 pound Brussels sprouts, trimmed and halved

* 1 tablespoon fresh thyme, minced

½ teaspoon kosher salt

⅛ teaspoon freshly ground black pepper

Serving Tip *If you want to make a sauce for the Brussels sprouts, remove the sprouts with a slotted spoon to a serving dish, then switch the cooker to the brown or sauté function. Stir in 1 tablespoon of apple cider vinegar and simmer the cider mixture until it is reduced by about half. Drizzle the sauce over the Brussels sprouts before serving.*

Vegetable Stock

PREP TIME: 15 MINUTES • COOK TIME: 20 MINUTES AT HIGH PRESSURE, NATURAL RELEASE

MAKES 8 CUPS A flavorful broth is the starting point for a myriad of soups, stews, sauces, and other recipes. And while it's convenient to buy broth concentrates or cartons of prepared broth, you can't beat the flavor of homemade. Plus, it's a great way to use up vegetable scraps. Save the trimmed ends of carrots, the inside parts of the celery head that wilt before you eat them, and unused parts of an onion when you didn't need a whole one for a recipe. Collect these scraps in a freezer bag, and when the bag is full, it's time to make stock. Make up a batch of this stock and freeze it.

GLUTEN-FREE

SOY-FREE

NUT-FREE

VEGAN

2 tablespoons extra-virgin olive oil

❋ 2 medium yellow onions, chopped into a few large pieces

❋ 4 garlic cloves, smashed

❋ 4 celery stalks, cut into several large pieces

❋ 4 carrots, peeled and cut into several large pieces

8 cups water

2 bay leaves

1 teaspoon dried thyme

❋ 5 fresh parsley sprigs

15 black peppercorns

½ teaspoon kosher salt

1. With the pressure cooker on the brown or sauté setting, heat the oil until it shimmers. Add the onions and sauté, stirring occasionally, until they soften and begin to brown, about 7 to 8 minutes. Add the garlic, celery, and carrots and sauté for 3 to 4 minutes more. Add the water, bay leaves, thyme, parsley, peppercorns, and salt.

2. Lock on the lid and set the timer for 20 minutes at high pressure. When the timer goes off, natural release the pressure.

3. Open the lid and pour the stock through a fine-mesh strainer into a bowl, removing and discarding all the solids. Cool before refrigerating or freezing.

Cooking Tip *Stock freezes beautifully in zip-top freezer bags. Measure 1- or 2-cup portions into a freezer bag, carefully squeeze most of the air out, seal (don't forget to label!), and freeze flat. To thaw, run the sealed bag under warm water to melt it enough to get it out of the bag, then transfer it to a vessel to thaw it on the stove or in the microwave.*

Chapter Three

ONE-POT WONDERS

BREAKFASTS

73

ONE-POT DINNERS

85

SOUPS AND STEWS

101

BREAKFASTS

74 Poached Eggs

75 Parmesan Coddled Eggs

76 Soft-Cooked Egg on Avocado Toast

77 Breakfast Custard for One

78 Pumpkin Oatmeal

79 Quinoa Porridge with Dried Fruit

80 Steel-Cut Oats with Brown Sugar, Cinnamon, and Almonds

81 Goat Cheese and Asparagus Breakfast Strata

82 French Toast Casserole

Poached Eggs

PREP TIME: 2 MINUTES • COOK TIME: 3 MINUTES AT LOW PRESSURE, QUICK RELEASE

SERVES 2 In culinary school, I learned how to make perfect poached eggs by dropping them into simmering water, but more than a decade later the skill now evades me and I end up with an overcooked mess. I was thrilled to master the technique of poaching eggs in a pressure cooker. You can use silicone egg cups, such as Poach Pods, which can be found in most kitchenware stores, or small glass custard cups—but the cooking process might take a minute longer.

GLUTEN-FREE

SOY-FREE

NUT-FREE

1 cup water

Cooking spray

✳ 2 eggs

Pinch kosher salt

Pinch freshly ground
 black pepper

1. Place a rack in the pot of a pressure cooker and add the water to the cooker. Spray the insides of two silicone egg poaching cups or heat-proof glass custard cups with cooking spray. Crack an egg into each cup and place the cups on the rack.

2. Lock on the lid and set the timer for 3 minutes at low pressure. When the timer goes off, quick release the pressure and open the lid. If the eggs are not quite as set as you like, replace the lid and let them sit in the hot cooker for an additional 1 to 2 minutes.

3. Turn the eggs out onto a plate or on a piece of toasted bread or English muffin. Sprinkle with the salt and pepper. Serve immediately.

Ingredient Tip *Traditionally, very fresh eggs are best when poaching, as the whites will hold together better. Since the egg is contained in a cup while being cooked in this recipe, this cooking method is a little more forgiving, although I still try to use eggs that are as fresh as possible.*

Parmesan Coddled Eggs

PREP TIME: 5 MINUTES • COOK TIME: 4 MINUTES AT LOW PRESSURE, QUICK RELEASE

SERVES 2 Coddled eggs are gently steam-cooked, ideally in an egg coddler—little ceramic pots with metal lids that screw on—designed expressly for the purpose. My eldest daughter, in particular, loves a coddled egg for breakfast, with toast soldiers for dipping, of course. Egg coddlers are easy to find at most kitchenware stores, and you can find vintage coddlers at flea markets and antique stores—I have a small collection I've found over the years. A glass custard cup or small ceramic ramekin works, too.

GLUTEN-FREE

SOY-FREE

NUT-FREE

1 tablespoon unsalted butter, room temperature

✴ 2 tablespoons finely grated Parmesan cheese

✴ 2 eggs

Pinch kosher salt

Pinch freshly ground black pepper

1 cup water

1. Using a paper towel or your clean fingers, generously rub the inside of two small glass or ceramic ramekins, or egg coddlers, with butter. Divide the Parmesan cheese between each ramekin, and turn and shake the ramekins to coat the bottom and sides with the cheese. Crack an egg into each ramekin, sprinkle with the salt and pepper, and cover each tightly with aluminum foil.

2. Place a rack in the pot of a pressure cooker. Add the water to the cooker and place the ramekins on the rack. Lock on the lid and set the timer for 4 minutes at low pressure. When the timer goes off, quick release the pressure and open the lid. Carefully remove the ramekins, uncover, and serve immediately.

Preparation Tip *Coddled eggs lend themselves to many variations. Try adding a dash of cream to the ramekin after you've cracked the egg in, or sprinkle the eggs with finely minced herbs, such as tarragon or chives, before cooking. The Parmesan cheese can be omitted if you're not a fan.*

Soft-Cooked Egg on Avocado Toast

PREP TIME: 7 MINUTES • COOK TIME: 3 MINUTES AT HIGH PRESSURE, QUICK RELEASE

SERVES 1 This nourishing dish is one of my favorite breakfasts: quick, easy, filling, and flavorful. Sometimes I'll add a few dashes of hot sauce to the avocado for a kick. Use this method to cook an egg any time you want a just-set white and a yolk that's still a bit runny. You can cook a bunch of eggs at a time and keep them in a bowl of warm water if you're cooking for a crowd.

SOY-FREE
NUT-FREE

½ cup water
✳ 1 egg
✳ 1 slice whole-wheat or multigrain bread
✳ ½ very ripe avocado
✳ 1 teaspoon freshly squeezed lemon juice
Dash kosher salt

Cooking Tip *This cooking method yields an egg with a set white but a runny yolk. For a yolk that is slightly more set, cook the egg for 4 minutes.*

1. Place a rack in the pot of a pressure cooker. Add the water to the cooker and place the egg, in its shell, on the rack. Lock on the lid and set the timer for 3 minutes at high pressure.

2. While the egg cooks, toast the bread in a toaster or toaster oven.

3. Using a spoon, scrape the avocado flesh into a small bowl. Add the lemon juice and salt and mash the avocado with the spoon until it is a creamy spread, but with a few chunks still remaining.

4. When the pressure cooker timer goes off, quick release the pressure, open the cooker, and remove the egg with a pair of tongs or a slotted spoon. Rinse it under cool water until just cool enough to handle. Peel the egg.

5. Spread the avocado mixture on the toasted bread. Place the egg on top of the avocado, and cut it in half. The yolk will be runny; let it spill out of the white onto the avocado. Serve immediately.

Breakfast Custard for One

PREP TIME: 7 MINUTES • COOK TIME: 5 MINUTES AT LOW PRESSURE, QUICK RELEASE

SERVES 1 Sometimes it's nice to treat yourself to a fancier breakfast, even if it's just you at the table (or in bed, who's judging?). This little custard is a decadent way to start the day, perhaps along with a buttered English muffin and a few pieces of fruit. For variety, try changing up the herbs, or even add a tablespoon of chopped cooked vegetables, like spinach or asparagus. Swiss cheese is nice to use as well, or try crumbling a stilton into the custard, which will give it a creamier texture.

SOY-FREE
NUT-FREE

Unsalted butter for greasing
☀ 1 egg
☀ ¼ cup whole milk
  ¼ teaspoon kosher salt
  ⅛ teaspoon freshly ground
    black pepper
☀ 2 tablespoons shredded
    sharp Cheddar cheese
☀ 1 tablespoon fresh
    minced chives
  1 cup water
☀ ½ tablespoon bread crumbs

Cooking Tip *You can make as many of these individual custards as will fit in your pressure cooker—mine will hold four at once. It might take a little longer for the pot to come to pressure, but the same cooking time of 5 minutes applies. I like to customize them for everyone I'm feeding with different types of cheeses or herbs.*

1. Rub the butter over the interior of a 4-ounce ramekin or glass baking dish. Set aside.

2. In a small bowl, whisk together the egg, milk, salt, and pepper. Stir in the cheese and chives. Pour the mixture into the ramekin.

3. Place the rack in the pressure cooker pot and add the water. Place the ramekin on the rack and sprinkle the top of the egg mixture with the bread crumbs. By sprinkling on the bread crumbs just before cooking, they don't sink into the egg mixture.

4. Lock on the lid and set the timer for 5 minutes at low pressure. When the timer goes off, quick release the pressure, carefully remove the ramekin from the pressure cooker, and serve immediately.

Pumpkin Oatmeal

PREP TIME: 5 MINUTES • COOK TIME: 4 MINUTES AT HIGH PRESSURE, NATURAL RELEASE

SERVES 4 In the fall, when it seems like everything is pumpkin spice–flavored, I can't resist stirring a little pumpkin into my oatmeal. It makes an everyday breakfast a little richer. What's more, it makes oatmeal even healthier: pumpkin purée is a good source of fiber, vitamin A, iron, and beta carotene. If you have a jar of pumpkin pie spice on hand, use a teaspoon of it in place of the other spices in this recipe.

1. In a heat-proof glass bowl that will fit inside the pressure cooker, combine the oats, pumpkin purée, brown sugar, 1½ cups of water, milk, cinnamon, ginger, and nutmeg. Place a rack in the pressure cooker pot and add the remaining 1 cup of water to the pot. Place the bowl on the rack

2. Lock on the lid, and set the timer for 4 minutes at high pressure. When the timer goes off, turn off the cooker and natural release the pressure. If, after 10 minutes, the pressure hasn't completely been released, quick release the remaining pressure. Carefully remove the bowl from inside the cooker and stir in any liquid on the surface. Serve hot.

GLUTEN-FREE
SOY-FREE
NUT-FREE

- 2 cups rolled oats
- ½ cup pumpkin purée
- 3 tablespoons brown sugar
- 2½ cups water, divided
- 1 cup whole or part-skim milk
- 1 teaspoon ground cinnamon
- ½ teaspoon ground ginger
- Dash nutmeg

Ingredient Tip *Choose regular rolled oats (sometimes called old-fashioned oats), rather than quick-cooking oats, for this recipe. Also, make sure to buy plain pumpkin purée, rather than pumpkin pie filling.*

Quinoa Porridge with Dried Fruit

PREP TIME: 7 MINUTES • COOK TIME: 5 MINUTES AT HIGH PRESSURE, NATURAL RELEASE

SERVES 2 If you're a fan of oatmeal, change things up and try quinoa instead. Because it's high in protein, it'll keep you full all morning long. I use a combination of chopped dates and dried cranberries, but you can change the flavor profile of this dish by what fruit and spices you add. For instance, dried apricots and ginger go great together, or dried apples pair well with cinnamon, nutmeg, and brown sugar, making the porridge taste almost like apple pie!

1. Place a rack into the pot of the pressure cooker. Add 1 cup of water to the pot.

2. In a heat-proof glass 1-quart bowl, combine the quinoa, the remaining ½ cup of water, milk, diced fruit, and cinnamon. Stir with a spoon to combine and scrape down any stray pieces of quinoa from the sides of the bowl. Place the bowl on the rack.

3. Lock on the lid and set the timer for 5 minutes at high pressure. When the timer goes off, natural release the pressure for 10 minutes, then quick release any remaining pressure. Stir the quinoa, then stir in the maple syrup. Serve hot.

GLUTEN-FREE
SOY-FREE
NUT-FREE

1½ cups water, divided
* ½ cup white quinoa
* ½ cup milk
* ¼ cup diced dried fruit
  ¼ teaspoon ground cinnamon
* ½ tablespoon maple syrup or brown sugar

Ingredient Tip *Quinoa recipes often call for rinsing the quinoa first to remove its naturally bitter coating. But packaged quinoa is scrubbed at the factory first, so this step can usually be avoided. Check the instructions on the packaging, and if it calls for the quinoa to be rinsed before cooking, definitely do it.*

Steel-Cut Oats with Brown Sugar, Cinnamon, and Almonds

PREP TIME: 8 MINUTES • COOK TIME: 10 MINUTES AT HIGH PRESSURE, NATURAL RELEASE

SERVES 2 Until I got my pressure cooker, steel-cut oats were a luxury we only enjoyed on the weekends, since they take nearly an hour to prepare on the stove. I love that this recipe can be prepared even on a busy weekday morning. Steel-cut oats have such a different texture from rolled oats: the little grains practically pop in your mouth! Be sure you use regular steel-cut oats, not the quick-cook variety.

GLUTEN-FREE
SOY-FREE

1 tablespoon unsalted butter
* 1 cup steel-cut oats
* 1 cup whole or part-skim milk, divided
2 tablespoons brown sugar
1 teaspoon ground cinnamon
½ teaspoon vanilla extract
* ¼ cup slivered almonds, toasted

1. With the pressure cooker on the sauté or brown setting, melt the butter. When it melts, add the oats and toast them, stirring frequently, for 2 to 3 minutes, until they're fragrant. Add 2 cups of water and ½ cup of milk, the brown sugar, and the cinnamon. Stir to combine.

2. Lock on the lid and set the timer for 10 minutes at high pressure. When the timer goes off, turn off the cooker and natural release for 10 minutes, then quick release any remaining pressure. Open the cooker and stir the liquid back into the oats. If it's still soupy, cover the cooker and let the oats sit for 5 minutes.

3. Stir in as much of the remaining ½ cup of milk as desired and the vanilla extract. Serve hot, sprinkled with the toasted almonds.

Cooking Tip *I've purposely left this recipe basic because it's ripe for personalization. Top with a drizzle of maple syrup, a few teaspoons of Quick Berry Compote (p. 143, as shown p. 72), some chopped dates, toasted walnuts, or any other fresh or dried fruits, nuts, or sweeteners you'd like.*

Goat Cheese and Asparagus Breakfast Strata

PREP TIME: 15 MINUTES • COOK TIME: 20 MINUTES AT LOW PRESSURE, NATURAL RELEASE

SERVES 4 Use a crusty bread, such as a baguette, for this savory breakfast dish. It's best for it to be a bit stale. If you're using cooked asparagus, see Steamed Asparagus, Four Ways (page 54) to make it quickly in your pressure cooker. This is a great recipe to assemble the night before and refrigerate. Let the cold dish sit out for an hour before cooking, and make sure the dish can withstand changes in temperature so it doesn't crack.

1. In a 2-quart tempered glass baking dish that fits into the pot of your pressure cooker, rub the bottom and insides with 1 tablespoon of butter. Arrange a layer of the bread on the bottom of the dish. Sprinkle half the goat cheese and asparagus over the bread. Place another layer of bread in the dish and top it with the remaining goat cheese and asparagus. Top this with any remaining bread to fill to the top of the dish. Set aside.

2. In a medium bowl, lightly whisk the eggs. Whisk in the milk, salt, mustard, and pepper. Pour the mixture over the bread and use a wooden spoon or spatula to press the bread down to soak it with the egg mixture. Let it sit for 5 minutes to allow the bread to absorb the eggs.

3. Place the rack inside the pressure cooker pot. Pour the water into the pot. Cut the remaining 1 tablespoon of butter into small pieces and dot them over the top of the casserole. Carefully put the casserole dish on the rack inside the pressure cooker.

4. Lock on the lid and set the timer for 20 minutes at low pressure. When the timer goes off, natural release the pressure for 10 minutes. Quick release any remaining pressure and carefully take the dish out of the pressure cooker. Serve hot.

SOY-FREE
NUT-FREE

2 tablespoons unsalted butter, divided
* 1 small baguette, cut into 1-inch chunks
* 4 ounces goat cheese, crumbled
* 8 ounces cooked asparagus, cut into 1-inch chunks (or use thawed frozen asparagus)
* 3 eggs
* 1½ cups whole milk
¼ teaspoon kosher salt
¼ teaspoon dry mustard
⅛ teaspoon freshly ground black pepper
1 cup water

Cooking Tip *You can use this recipe as a master guide to change the flavor profile. Try it with cheddar cheese and cooked broccoli, or provolone and sautéed mushrooms.*

French Toast Casserole

PREP TIME: 15 MINUTES • COOK TIME: 20 MINUTES AT LOW PRESSURE, NATURAL RELEASE

SERVES 4 This is a reimagined version of French toast, in casserole form. It's got all the right flavors: maple, cinnamon, butter, and more. It's a great way to use stale bread. I like using good-quality bakery white bread, but brioche or cinnamon raisin bread would also be delicious options. You can even assemble this the night before and refrigerate it, covered. Make sure to use a tempered glass dish so that it won't crack with the temperature change, and set it out about an hour before you cook it.

1. Rub the bottom and insides of a 2-quart tempered glass baking dish that fits into the pot of your pressure cooker with 1 tablespoon of butter. Pile the bread cubes in the dish, and set aside.

2. In a medium bowl, lightly whisk the eggs. Whisk in the milk, maple syrup, vanilla, cinnamon, and salt. Pour the mixture over the bread and use a wooden spoon or spatula to press the bread down to soak it with the egg mixture. Let it sit for 5 minutes to allow the bread to absorb the eggs.

SOY-FREE

NUT-FREE

2 tablespoons unsalted butter, divided

❋ 8 slices stale white bread, crusts removed, cut into 1-inch cubes

❋ 3 eggs

❋ 1½ cups whole milk

❋ ¼ cup maple syrup

1 tablespoon vanilla extract

1 teaspoon ground cinnamon

⅛ teaspoon kosher salt

1 cup water

3. Place the rack inside the pressure cooker pot. Pour the water into the pot. Cut the remaining 1 tablespoon of butter into small pieces and dot them over the top of the casserole. Carefully put the casserole dish on the rack inside the pressure cooker.

4. Lock on the lid and set the timer for 20 minutes at low pressure. When the timer goes off, natural release the pressure for 10 minutes. Quick release any remaining pressure and carefully take the dish out of the pressure cooker. Serve hot.

Preparation Tip *The bread should be stale so that it can absorb more of the custard. If your bread still feels fresh and moist, place it directly on the rack in a 250˚F oven for 5 minutes, until it feels dry to the touch but is not toasted.*

ONE-POT DINNERS

86   Arugula Risotto

87   Risotto with Peas

88   Leek and Asparagus Risotto

90   Korean Sushi Bowls with Egg

91   Quick Green Posole

92   Harvest Ratatouille

93   Green Thai Tofu and Veggie Curry

94   Indian Chickpea Curry

95   Spaghetti Squash with Pesto and
Fresh Mozzarella

96   Speedy Scratch Mac n' Cheese

97   Baked Eggs with Artichokes in Tomato Sauce

98   Cheesy Noodle "Helper"

99   Peas and Paneer in Indian Sauce

Arugula Risotto

PREP TIME: 15 MINUTES • COOK TIME: 10 MINUTES AT HIGH PRESSURE, QUICK RELEASE

SERVES 4 Risotto without all the stirring? Yep! While a real Italian might scoff, I think that an electric pressure cooker makes a reasonable facsimile to an authentic Italian risotto. The process starts the same way—sautéing the aromatics and toasting the rice—but instead of ladling a bit of broth into the rice at a time, it's added all at once, and the pressure cooker does the work of making creamy, toothsome rice. In this version, peppery baby arugula is stirred in at the very end.

GLUTEN-FREE
SOY-FREE
NUT-FREE

2 tablespoons
    unsalted butter
✳ 1 shallot, finely minced
    1 tablespoon white
    wine vinegar
✳ 1½ cups Arborio rice
✳ 3 cups vegetarian chicken
    broth or vegetable broth
✳ ½ cup finely grated
    Parmesan cheese, plus
    more for serving
    ¼ teaspoon freshly ground
    black pepper
✳ 2 cups baby
    arugula, chopped

1. With the pressure cooker on the sauté or brown setting, melt the butter. Add the shallot and sauté, stirring frequently, until the shallots are softened and translucent, 4 to 5 minutes. Add the vinegar and the rice and sauté for 1 minute, stirring constantly, until the rice is coated with the butter and vinegar. Add the broth and stir to combine, scraping down any stray grains of rice from the sides of the pot.

2. Lock on the lid and set the timer for 10 minutes at high pressure. When the timer goes off, quick release the pressure and open the cooker.

3. Stir in the cheese, pepper, and arugula. Replace the lid and let it sit for 1 to 2 minutes, until the arugula has wilted. Serve immediately, topped with additional Parmesan cheese if desired.

Ingredient Tip *If you don't like the peppery bite of arugula, you can substitute baby spinach or baby kale in this recipe. Or, if you want to get more exotic, try using watercress.*

Risotto with Peas

PREP TIME: 10 MINUTES ● COOK TIME: 11 MINUTES AT HIGH PRESSURE, QUICK RELEASE

SERVES 4 Mushroom broth lends richness and lots of earthy flavor to this risotto, which is studded with fresh peas. I like to garnish it with a handful of fresh chopped parsley for added bright flavor and a generous sprinkling of additional Parmesan cheese, too. If you use fresh peas instead of frozen, they will take the same amount of time to cook—1 minute at high pressure.

GLUTEN-FREE
SOY-FREE
NUT-FREE

1 cup water

✲ 2 cups frozen peas

2 tablespoons unsalted butter

✲ 1 shallot, minced

✲ 1½ cups Arborio rice

✲ 3 cups mushroom broth

✲ ½ cup finely grated Parmesan cheese, plus more for serving

¼ teaspoon freshly ground black pepper

1. Add the water to the pressure cooker pot. Place a steamer insert in the cooker and place the peas in the insert.

2. Lock on the lid and set the timer for 1 minute. When the timer goes off, quick release the pressure and open the lid. Carefully lift the steamer basket out of the cooker and transfer the peas to a bowl. Cover the bowl loosely with aluminum foil to keep the peas warm. Pour the water out of the pot and wipe it dry.

3. With the pressure cooker on the sauté or brown setting, melt the butter. When it's hot, add the shallot and sauté, stirring frequently, until softened and translucent, about 5 minutes. Add the rice and sauté it for 1 minute, stirring constantly, until the grains are coated with the butter. Add the broth and stir to combine, scraping down any stray rice grains from the sides of the pot.

4. Lock on the lid and set the timer for 10 minutes at high pressure. When the timer goes off, quick release the pressure and remove the lid. Stir in the cheese, pepper, and warm peas. Serve immediately, topped with additional Parmesan cheese if desired.

Leek and Asparagus Risotto

PREP TIME: 15 MINUTES • COOK TIME: 11 MINUTES AT HIGH PRESSURE, QUICK RELEASE

SERVES 4 This light risotto recipe is ideal for spring when asparagus is at its peak, but can be made with frozen asparagus, too. It's also nice with green beans, peapods, or artichoke hearts. Leeks, with their mellow flavor and melty texture, make an ideal aromatic base for any risotto. Be sure to wash the inside layers of the leek well, as they can trap dirt. I usually cut the leek in half from root to tip, then pull each layer apart to rinse under cool running water.

1. Place a steamer insert in the cooker and add the water to the pot. Place the asparagus in the steamer insert.

2. Lock on the lid and set the timer for 1 minute. When the timer goes off, quick release the pressure and open the lid. Use tongs to transfer the asparagus to a bowl. Cover loosely with aluminum foil and set aside. Remove the steamer insert and pour the water out. Wipe it dry with a paper towel.

3. With the pressure cooker on the sauté or brown setting, melt the butter. Add the leek and sauté, stirring frequently, until the leek is softened and translucent, about 5 minutes. Add the rice, sauté for 1 minute, stirring constantly, until the rice is coated with the butter. Add the broth and stir to combine, scraping down any stray grains of rice from the sides of the pot.

GLUTEN-FREE
SOY-FREE
NUT-FREE

1 cup water

✳ 1 pound asparagus, trimmed and cut into 1-inch pieces

2 tablespoons unsalted butter

✳ 1 leek, white part only, finely chopped

✳ 1½ cups Arborio rice

✳ 3 cups vegetarian chicken broth

✳ ½ cup finely grated Parmesan cheese, plus more for serving

¼ teaspoon freshly ground black pepper

4. Lock on the lid and set the timer for 10 minutes at high pressure. When the timer goes off, quick release the pressure and open the cooker.

5. Stir in the cheese, pepper, and warm asparagus. Serve immediately, topped with additional Parmesan cheese if desired.

Ingredient Tip *Although it won't have the same crisp-tender texture as fresh, you can use frozen asparagus in this recipe. Thaw the stalks and cut them into 1-inch pieces. Instead of steaming at the beginning, stir the thawed asparagus into the cooked risotto as in step 3. Cover the cooker and let it sit for 3 to 4 minutes to warm the asparagus before serving.*

Korean Sushi Bowls with Egg

PREP TIME: 10 MINUTES • COOK TIME: 3 MINUTES AT HIGH PRESSURE, NATURAL RELEASE

SERVES 4 Rice bowls topped with fresh-tasting, healthy ingredients are a great one-pot dinner. This one combines Japanese and Korean flavors—you've got the sushi-style rice, avocado, and seaweed, and the tangy bite of kimchi, a Korean fermented vegetable condiment that usually involves cabbage, radish, and other veggies. You can find it in Asian markets or in the international food aisle of a well-stocked supermarket. If you don't like kimchi or have trouble finding it, substitute thinly sliced cucumber tossed with seasoned rice vinegar and a pinch each of sugar and salt.

GLUTEN-FREE
NUT-FREE

* 1½ cups sushi rice
1½ cups water
1 tablespoon seasoned rice vinegar
* 1 cup prepared kimchi
* 2 avocados, sliced
* 1 (0.35 ounce) package seaweed snack or 4 sheets dried nori, cut into strips
* 4 soft-cooked eggs, kept warm

1. In a fine-mesh strainer, rinse the rice well, rubbing handfuls of the grains between your fingers. Rinse the rice until the water nearly runs clear, then drain it well. Place the rice and the water in the pressure cooker pot.

2. Lock on the lid and set the timer for 3 minutes at high pressure. When the timer goes off, natural release the pressure for 10 minutes, then quick release any remaining pressure. Open the lid and sprinkle the vinegar over the rice. Fluff the rice with a fork to distribute the vinegar.

3. Divide the rice between four bowls. Arrange the kimchi, avocado slices, and a handful of the seaweed on top of the rice. Peel the eggs and slice each in half over the ingredients in the bowl. Serve immediately.

Preparation Tip *Follow the instructions for Soft-Cooked Egg on Avocado Toast (page 76) to make a perfectly cooked egg for this recipe; leave the eggs in their shell until you assemble the bowls. But any kind of egg in which the yolk is still runny, such as a fried or poached egg (page 74), can be used instead of the soft-cooked egg. The creamy yolk will mix with the rice and other ingredients, serving as a rich sauce.*

Quick Green Posole

PREP TIME: 10 MINUTES • COOK TIME: 3 MINUTES AT LOW PRESSURE, QUICK RELEASE

SERVES 4 When I visit my mom, who lives in Santa Fe, I try to eat as much posole as I can. This spicy, flavorful New Mexican stew made from hominy is rare to find anywhere else. And vegetarians are often disappointed to find that it's nearly always made with a ham hock or another pork cut to give it flavor. I developed this meatless version to have a brighter, zestier flavor, thanks to the fresh, tangy flavor of tomatillos.

1. Put the tomatillos, jalapeño, and onion in a blender and pulse to chop all the ingredients into a chunky purée. Pour the mixture into the pressure cooker pot. Add the hominy, vegetable broth, cumin, chili powder, garlic powder, oregano, and salt.

2. Lock on the lid on the pressure cooker and set the timer for 3 minutes at low pressure. When the timer goes off, quick release the pressure. Stir the mixture to recombine, add additional salt if needed, and serve immediately.

GLUTEN-FREE
SOY-FREE
NUT-FREE
VEGAN

- 6 ounces (about 5) tomatillos, hulled, washed, and quartered
- ½ jalapeño, seeded and ribs removed, roughly chopped
- 1 small yellow onion, roughly chopped
- 2 (15-ounce) cans hominy, drained
- 1 cup vegetable broth
  1 teaspoon ground cumin
  ½ teaspoon chili powder
  1 teaspoon garlic powder
  ½ teaspoon dried oregano
  ¼ teaspoon kosher salt, plus more for seasoning

Serving Tip *Posole is delicious topped with a dollop of sour cream or some diced avocado.*

Harvest Ratatouille

PREP TIME: 15 MINUTES • COOK TIME: 3 MINUTES AT HIGH PRESSURE, QUICK RELEASE

SERVES 4 The name of this stew derives from the French word for "to stir up." I like to think of French housewives patrolling their gardens in late summer to see what was ready to be stirred into this rustic stew. It's definitely a dish that can be made year-round, and I think it tastes best when it's made from produce procured at my local farmers' market. I like to serve it as a soup, alongside a grilled baguette rubbed with olive oil and garlic, or atop a bed of pasta noodles.

GLUTEN-FREE
SOY-FREE
NUT-FREE
VEGAN

2 tablespoons extra-virgin olive oil, divided
* 2 large yellow onions, diced
1 teaspoon garlic powder
1 teaspoon dried thyme
1 teaspoon dried oregano
½ teaspoon kosher salt, plus more if needed
* 1 eggplant, cut into 1-inch chunks
* 2 red bell peppers, seeded and diced
* 2 yellow squash, cut into 1-inch chunks
* 1 (28-ounce) can whole peeled tomatoes, in juice
¼ teaspoon freshly ground black pepper

1. With the pressure cooker on the brown or sauté setting, heat 1 tablespoon of olive oil until it shimmers. Add the onions and sauté, stirring frequently, until they are softened and translucent, about 5 minutes. Stir in the garlic powder, thyme, oregano, and salt. Add the eggplant, bell peppers, and squash, and pour the tomatoes and their juices over the vegetables, without stirring.

2. Lock on the lid and set the timer for 3 minutes at high pressure. When the timer goes off, quick release the pressure. Gently stir the ingredients, drizzling in the remaining 1 tablespoon of olive oil and season with the black pepper and additional salt, if needed. Serve hot or warm.

Ingredient Tip *If you are sensitive to the bitterness of eggplant, try putting the cut eggplant chunks in a colander, tossing them with 2 tablespoons of kosher salt, and letting them sit for up to an hour. Then rinse the salt off and proceed with the recipe.*

Green Thai Tofu and Veggie Curry

PREP TIME: 15 MINUTES ● COOK TIME: 3 MINUTES AT HIGH PRESSURE, QUICK RELEASE

SERVES 4 Why bother to make your own curry sauce when the prepared sauces are so tasty? I pair this recipe with white or brown rice. Cook it first in your pressure cooker, then transfer it to a serving dish and keep it warm under aluminum foil. Wash out the pot and get started on the curry (or better yet, see if your pressure cooker manufacturer sells additional inner pots; they're handy to have when using your cooker for multiple dishes).

GLUTEN-FREE
NUT-FREE
VEGAN

* 1 (14-ounce) block extra-firm tofu
* 2 red bell peppers, seeded and sliced
* 1 red onion, sliced
* 8 ounces green beans, trimmed and cut into 1-inch pieces
* 1 (14-ounce) can prepared green curry

1. Slice the tofu in half lengthwise, then cut each piece into 1-inch cubes. Add the tofu, peppers, onion, and green beans to the pressure cooker pot. Pour the curry sauce over the tofu and vegetables and stir lightly to combine.

2. Lock on the lid and set the timer for 3 minutes at high pressure. When the timer goes off, quick release the pressure. Stir to combine, and serve immediately.

Cooking Tip *This sauce is thin, so it soaks nicely into a bed of rice. If you prefer a thicker sauce, use a slotted spoon to remove all the vegetables and tofu from the pot and simmer it on the brown or sauté setting for 5 minutes, until it has reduced and thickened slightly. Return all the vegetables back to the pot to warm up before serving.*

Indian Chickpea Curry

PREP TIME: 10 MINUTES • COOK TIME: 3 MINUTES AT HIGH PRESSURE, QUICK RELEASE

SERVES 4 I make a big batch of Basic Chickpeas (page 42) and keep portions of them in the freezer. This recipe is a great way to use them up. Red curry paste is a great way to make a flavorful curry sauce as good as you'd find in a restaurant—the paste has all the right spices and ingredients! Make a batch of Basic White Rice (page 26) or Basic Brown Rice (page 27) in your pressure cooker first and keep it warm in a covered serving bowl while you make the curry.

GLUTEN-FREE

SOY-FREE

NUT-FREE

VEGAN

1 tablespoon vegetable oil

* 1 medium yellow onion, sliced

* 2 tablespoons red curry paste

* 1 (13.5-ounce) can coconut milk

2 teaspoons cornstarch

* 2 cups canned chickpeas, drained and rinsed, or 2 cups Basic Chickpeas (page 42)

* 4 carrots, peeled and sliced on the diagonal into 1-inch pieces

Cooking Tip *Other vegetables that work well in this curry include cauliflower florets, broccoli florets, sliced bell pepper, green beans, peas, and sliced zucchini.*

1. With the pressure cooker on the brown or sauté setting, heat the vegetable oil until it shimmers. Add the onion and sauté, stirring frequently, until it is softened and translucent, about 5 minutes. Stir in the curry paste and sauté, stirring constantly, for 1 minute. Stir in the coconut milk.

2. Place the cornstarch in a small bowl. Add a spoonful or two of warm liquid from the pot to the bowl and use a fork or spoon to make a loose paste. Stir the cornstarch mixture back into the pot. Add the chickpeas and carrots to the pot.

3. Lock on the lid and set the timer for 3 minutes at high pressure. When the timer goes off, quick release the pressure. Stir the curry and serve hot.

Spaghetti Squash with Pesto and Fresh Mozzarella

PREP TIME: 10 MINUTES • COOK TIME: 7 MINUTES AT HIGH PRESSURE, QUICK RELEASE

SERVES 4 Spaghetti squash lends itself well to a range of flavors, and people who can't eat actual pasta like to use it in place of the real thing since it has a similar appearance and texture. That's what I've done here, where I've created a riff on the classic Italian flavors of a Caprese salad, with basil, tomatoes, and mozzarella. I call for prepared pesto for convenience, but if you happen to have a boatload of basil from your garden, by all means make homemade pesto!

1. Slice the stem end off the spaghetti squash and cut it into quarters. Use a spoon to scoop out the seeds and the pulp.

2. Place a rack or a steamer insert in the pressure cooker pot and add the water to the pot. Place the squash on the rack or steamer, cut-side down. The squash can be layered on top of each other, but shouldn't fill the pot more than two-thirds full. If it doesn't all fit, cook it in two batches.

3. Lock on the lid and set the timer for 7 minutes at high pressure. When the timer goes off, quick release the pressure, open the cooker, and remove the squash with tongs.

4. When the squash is cool enough to handle, use a fork to scrape the squash into strands, transferring them to a large bowl. Spoon the pesto over the squash, and use tongs to toss the squash, distributing the pesto to evenly coat the squash. Add the mozzarella and cherry tomatoes, and toss to combine. Serve warm or at room temperature.

GLUTEN-FREE
SOY-FREE

- 2 (3-pound) spaghetti squash
- 1 cup water
- ½ cup prepared pesto
- 8 ounces fresh mozzarella cheese, cubed
- 2 cups quartered cherry tomatoes

Ingredient Tip *When I buy prepared pesto, I first check the refrigerator section of my supermarket to see if they have fresh pesto available, rather than the shelf-stable jarred pesto. Fresh pesto, sold in plastic tubs, has a brighter flavor and is closer to homemade.*

Speedy Scratch Mac n' Cheese

PREP TIME: 10 MINUTES • COOK TIME: 5 MINUTES AT HIGH PRESSURE, QUICK RELEASE

SERVES 4 TO 6 My foodie friend Janet Zimmerman is just as obsessed with pressure cooking as I am—in fact, she, too, has written pressure cooker cookbooks. She shared with me her favorite recipe for macaroni and cheese, and it's delicious! You'll love this recipe, which is ready in the same amount of time it takes to cook that box of pasta on the stove.

1. In the pot of the pressure cooker, add the macaroni, ¾ cup of evaporated milk, water, salt, and dried mustard. Stir to combine.

2. Lock on the lid and set the timer for 5 minutes at high pressure.

3. Meanwhile, in a small bowl, whisk the egg. Add the remaining ¼ cup of evaporated milk and whisk to combine.

4. Place the grated cheese in a medium bowl and sprinkle the cornstarch over the cheese. Toss to coat.

5. When the pressure cooker timer goes off, quick release the pressure. Test the macaroni, if it is not quite done, switch the setting to sauté or brown, and simmer it for 1 to 2 minutes, covered, until tender.

6. If you haven't switched the setting, switch the setting to sauté or brown and add the milk-egg mixture and a large handful of cheese. Stir to melt the cheese. Continue adding the cheese in several handfuls, stirring until it completely melts with each addition. Serve immediately.

SOY-FREE
NUT-FREE

- 8 ounces elbow macaroni
- 1 cup evaporated milk, divided
- 1¼ cups water
- 1½ teaspoons kosher salt
- 1 teaspoon dried mustard
- 1 egg
- 8 ounces extra-sharp Cheddar cheese, grated
- 1½ teaspoons cornstarch

Cooking Tip *For baked-style macaroni, transfer the finished mac 'n cheese to an ovenproof serving dish, sprinkle it with about ½ cup of bread crumbs (try mixing them with a few table-spoons of grated Parmesan cheese for a treat!) and put it under a preheated broiler for several minutes until the top browns and bubbles.*

Baked Eggs with Artichokes in Tomato Sauce

PREP TIME: 7 MINUTES • COOK TIME: 4 MINUTES AT HIGH PRESSURE, QUICK RELEASE

SERVES 2 I don't know if the concept of simmering eggs in tomato sauce originated in Italy, the Middle East, or elsewhere. What I do know is that it makes for a delicious light dinner alongside a simple green salad. If you like things spicy, you can make a variation known as "eggs in purgatory" by stirring ¼ teaspoon, or more, red pepper flakes into each ramekin of tomato sauce before adding the eggs.

GLUTEN-FREE

SOY-FREE

NUT-FREE

1 cup water

❋ 1½ cups Hearty Tomato Sauce (page 137) or jarred marinara sauce

❋ ½ cup chopped jarred artichoke hearts, drained

❋ 2 eggs

❋ 2 tablespoons finely grated Parmesan cheese

❋ 2 slices toasted bread

1 tablespoon extra-virgin olive oil

¼ teaspoon kosher salt

⅛ teaspoon freshly ground black pepper

1. Place the rack inside the pressure cooker pot. Add the water to the pot.

2. Divide the marinara sauce between two large (about 1½ cups size) ramekins. Stir in the artichoke hearts. Break an egg into the middle of each ramekin and sprinkle each with the Parmesan cheese. Place the ramekins on the rack in the pressure cooker.

3. Lock on the lid and set the timer for 4 minutes at high pressure.

4. While the eggs are cooking, brush the toasted bread with the olive oil.

5. When the timer goes off, quick release the pressure. Carefully remove the ramekins from the pot and season them with the salt and pepper. Serve immediately, with the toasts for dipping.

Cheesy Noodle "Helper"

PREP TIME: 5 MINUTES • COOK TIME: 4 MINUTES AT HIGH PRESSURE, QUICK RELEASE

SERVES 4 This meal is reminiscent of one of those boxed "helper" dinners that busy parents rely on to get dinner on the table. This vegetarian version is just as easy to prepare, and even quicker. Use your favorite meatless crumble in it (I'm a fan of Gardein crumbles). This recipe is great for a game-watching party; it can be doubled if all the ingredients fill your pressure cooker no more than half full.

1. Combine the macaroni, vegetable broth, water, and olive oil in the pot of the pressure cooker.

2. Lock on the lid and set the timer for 4 minutes at high pressure. When the timer goes off, quick release the pressure. Remove the lid and stir the pasta to break it up.

3. With the pressure cooker on the sauté or brown setting, add the tomatoes, meatless crumbles, and cheese. Stir the mixture until the tomato sauce and crumbles are heated through and the cheese is melted. Serve hot.

NUT-FREE

* 1½ cups elbow macaroni
* 1 cup vegetable broth
  ½ cup water
  1 tablespoon extra-virgin olive oil
* 1 can mild tomatoes and peppers, such as Ro-Tel
* 1½ cups meatless crumbles
* 1 cup (about 2 ounces) grated Cheddar cheese

Cooking Tip *When you make pasta, if you find liquid sputters out of the steam vent when you quick release the pressure, try placing a piece of parchment paper on top of the pasta. Cut a piece into a round just slightly smaller than the interior of the pressure cooker pot. After you've combined your pasta and water, rest the parchment over the mixture and proceed with the recipe. The parchment will keep the cooking liquid from foaming or spraying.*

Peas and Paneer in Indian Sauce

PREP TIME: 15 MINUTES • COOK TIME: 4 MINUTES AT HIGH PRESSURE, QUICK RELEASE

SERVES 4 Paneer is India's version of cottage cheese, but it is firm and chewy, similar in texture to tofu. Using one of the many tasty and high-quality jarred Indian sauces available makes preparing this dish so much easier than trying to create your own sauce with the myriad spices and seasonings needed. Any masala sauce or Indian butter sauce will work. I'm a fan of the sauces made by Patak's Original or Maya Kaimal. Ghee is clarified butter with all the milkfat removed. It's shelf-stable and can be found in the baking or international food aisle of the supermarket.

GLUTEN-FREE
SOY-FREE
NUT-FREE

2 tablespoons unsalted butter or ghee

* 1 (10-ounce package) paneer cheese, cut into cubes

* 1 small yellow onion, thinly sliced

* 1 (12.5-ounce jar) Indian simmer sauce, such as butter masala or tikka masala

* 1 (10-ounce) package frozen peas

* ¼ cup chopped fresh cilantro

Cooking Tip *To make a vegan version of this recipe, use firm tofu instead of cheese and oil in place of the butter. Make sure that the simmer sauce you use is vegan as well.*

1. With the pressure cooker on brown or sauté, heat the butter until it melts and shimmers. Working in batches if necessary, lightly brown the paneer cubes on all sides. Use a slotted spoon or tongs to remove the paneer cubes from the pot, and set them aside on a plate or in a shallow bowl.

2. Add the onion to the pot and sauté, stirring frequently, until it is softened and beginning to brown, about 5 minutes. Stir in the sauce, frozen peas, and paneer cubes.

3. Lock on the lid and set the timer for 4 minutes at high pressure. When the timer goes off, quick release the pressure. Remove the lid and gently stir the mixture. Sprinkle with the cilantro and serve hot or warm.

SOUPS AND STEWS

102   Creamy Asparagus Soup

103   Moroccan Chickpea Stew

104   Tomato Soup, Chunky or Creamy

105   Mushroom Soup

106   Tortilla Soup

107   Butternut Squash Soup with Coconut and Ginger

108   Cheesy Cauliflower Soup

109   Rosemary Potato-Leek Soup

110   Black Bean Soup with Chard and Veggie Sausage

111   Lentil-Mushroom Stew

112   Corn Chowder

113   French Onion Soup

114   Hoppin' John

115   Classic Chili

116   Quick Quinoa Chili

117   White Bean Chili

Creamy Asparagus Soup

PREP TIME: 15 MINUTES • COOK TIME: 10 MINUTES AT HIGH PRESSURE, QUICK RELEASE

SERVES 4 I love to serve this velvety soup in the spring and early summer when asparagus is at its peak, but it's also excellent prepared with frozen asparagus. For a special occasion, drizzle it with a bit of truffle oil just before serving or set aside a few of the asparagus tips to steam and use as a garnish. See the tip on trimming asparagus on page 54. This soup makes a great accompaniment to a quiche or an upscale grilled cheese sandwich.

1. Set the pressure cooker on brown or sauté, and melt the butter, tilting to coat the bottom of the pot. Add the shallots and sauté until translucent, about 5 minutes. Add the asparagus pieces, vegetable stock, and thyme.

2. Lock on the lid and set the timer for 10 minutes at high pressure. When the timer goes off, quick release the pressure and open the lid.

3. Allow the mixture to cool for a few minutes. Then use an immersion blender to purée the mixture until smooth, or transfer the mixture to the jar of a blender and purée the soup until it is smooth (make sure to vent the lid slightly to allow steam to escape). Stir in the cream and lemon juice, and season with salt and pepper. Serve hot.

GLUTEN-FREE
SOY-FREE
NUT-FREE

2 tablespoons unsalted butter

❋ 2 shallots, minced

❋ 2 pounds fresh asparagus, trimmed and cut into 1-inch pieces

❋ 2 cups vegetable stock

1 teaspoon dried thyme

❋ ½ cup heavy (whipping) cream

❋ 1 tablespoon freshly squeezed lemon juice

Salt

Freshly ground black pepper

Serving Tip *This is a delightful soup to serve for a special brunch or lunch. Garnish each bowl with a few asparagus tips, thin slices of radish, fresh dill, hazelnut pieces, and perhaps a few pomegranate seeds.*

Moroccan Chickpea Stew

PREP TIME: 10 MINUTES • COOK TIME: 4 MINUTES AT HIGH PRESSURE, QUICK RELEASE

SERVES 6 Redolent of exotic spices, this thick stew is just the thing on a cold winter's night. It's great on its own, perhaps with some fresh pita on the side to sop up the broth, or spooned over some Basic Brown Rice (page 27). It's a great way to use up a stash of Basic Chickpeas (page 42), but you can use canned if you have them on hand.

GLUTEN-FREE

SOY-FREE

NUT-FREE

VEGAN

2 tablespoons vegetable oil

* 1 medium yellow onion, diced

½ teaspoon garlic powder

1 tablespoon Moroccan spice blend (see tip)

* 1 (14.5-ounce) can diced tomatoes, with juice

* 3 medium carrots, peeled and sliced into ¾-inch coins

* 4 cups canned chickpeas, rinsed and drained, or 4 cups Basic Chickpeas (page 42)

* 2 cups vegetable broth

1. With the pressure cooker on the brown or sauté setting, heat the vegetable oil until it shimmers. Add the onion and sauté, stirring frequently, until it is softened and translucent, about 5 minutes. Stir in the garlic powder and spice blend and cook, stirring constantly, for about 30 seconds. Add the tomatoes, carrots, chickpeas, and vegetable broth. Stir to combine.

2. Lock on the lid and set the timer for 4 minutes at high pressure. When the timer goes off, quick release the pressure and remove the lid. Stir the stew and serve hot.

Ingredient Tip *Moroccan spice blend is available in the spice aisle of most supermarkets (McCormick's makes a version) or at specialty food stores. If you can't find it or want to make your own, stir together 1 teaspoon each of cumin and ground ginger, ½ teaspoon each of ground cinnamon and turmeric, and ¼ teaspoon of ground cayenne pepper or white pepper.*

Tomato Soup, Chunky or Creamy

PREP TIME: 10 MINUTES • COOK TIME: 15 MINUTES AT HIGH PRESSURE, NATURAL RELEASE

SERVES 6 If I had to assign a taste to my childhood, it would be canned tomato soup, usually accompanied by buttered toast or a grilled American cheese sandwich (of course!). This homemade tomato soup has a few more steps in it but is well worth the effort for its fresher taste and healthier profile. I like to purée it so it's velvety smooth, but many people like it chunky, so feel free to enjoy it either way.

GLUTEN-FREE
SOY-FREE
NUT-FREE

2 tablespoons unsalted butter

* 1½ cups mirepoix-style vegetable blend (diced onion, carrots, celery)

* 1 (28-ounce) can crushed tomatoes

½ teaspoon garlic powder

* 2 cups low-sodium vegetable broth

1 bay leaf

½ teaspoon kosher salt

¼ teaspoon freshly ground black pepper

* ½ cup heavy (whipping) cream

1. With the pressure cooker on the brown or sauté setting, heat the butter until it melts. Add the mirepoix blend and sauté, stirring frequently, until the vegetables are softened and translucent, about 5 minutes. Stir in the tomatoes, garlic powder, vegetable broth, bay leaf, salt, and pepper.

2. Lock on the lid and set the timer for 15 minutes. When the timer goes off, natural release for 10 minutes, then quick release any remaining pressure. Remove the lid and discard the bay leaf.

3. Use an immersion blender to purée the soup until it's smooth, or let the mixture cool slightly, transfer it to the jar of a blender, and purée, making sure to vent the lid so steam can escape. Stir in the heavy cream. Or, leave the soup unblended if you prefer a chunky, more rustic texture.

Ingredient Tip *Mirepoix (mir-pwa) is the French term for the classic combination of diced or minced onion, celery, and carrots and is the building block for many classic French soups and sauces. You can buy the three veggies already chopped and combined, which will save time in the kitchen. Or, you can make your own by combining two parts yellow onion with one part each carrot and celery, all diced to a uniform size.*

Mushroom Soup

PREP TIME: 15 MINUTES • COOK TIME: 20 MINUTES AT HIGH PRESSURE, NATURAL RELEASE

SERVES 4 TO 6 A good mushroom soup is ridiculously decadent. And even inexpensive button or cremini mushrooms make a rich, earthy-flavored soup. Of course you can sub in a few ounces of fancier mushrooms, such as morels, if you want to get extravagant. As with the Tomato Soup (page 104), a smooth or chunky soup is up to you. I like to ladle out a big scoop of mushrooms before puréeing the rest of the soup, then return the mushrooms back to the mix to give it a bit of texture.

SOY-FREE
NUT-FREE

2 tablespoons
unsalted butter
* 1 leek, white part only, diced
* 12 ounces white or cremini
mushrooms, sliced
* 2 tablespoons
all-purpose flour
* 4 cups low-sodium
vegetable or vegetarian
chicken-flavored broth
½ teaspoon dried thyme
* ½ cup heavy
(whipping) cream
½ teaspoon kosher salt
¼ teaspoon freshly ground
black pepper

1. With the pressure cooker on the brown or sauté setting, heat the butter until it melts and foams. Add the leeks and sauté, stirring occasionally, until they soften, about 5 minutes. Add the mushrooms and sauté, stirring occasionally, until softened, about 7 minutes. Sprinkle the flour over the mushrooms and continue cooking, stirring constantly, for 1 to 2 minutes. Gradually stir in the broth. Add the thyme.

2. Lock on the lid and set the timer for 20 minutes at high pressure. When the timer goes off, natural release the pressure and remove the lid.

3. Use an immersion blender to purée the soup or let it cool slightly and transfer it to a blender to purée, making sure to vent the lid so steam can escape. Stir in the cream, salt, and pepper. Serve hot.

Serving Tip *To make this soup even more special, finish it with a splash of good-quality sherry or a tiny drizzle of truffle oil.*

Tortilla Soup

PREP TIME: 15 MINUTES • COOK TIME: 12 MINUTES AT HIGH PRESSURE, NATURAL RELEASE

SERVES 4 TO 6 Corn tortillas serve two purposes in this soup: they thicken the soup, and they serve as a crispy garnish on top. I like to also set out a whole buffet of additional toppings, just like I do for chili: diced avocado, fresh cilantro, sour cream, and chopped scallions. If you want to give it more substance, add a 15-ounce can of black beans or hominy (drained and rinsed) along with the frozen corn.

GLUTEN-FREE
SOY-FREE
NUT-FREE
VEGAN

¼ cup vegetable oil
✹ 6 taco-size soft corn tortillas, divided
1¼ teaspoons kosher salt, divided
✹ 1 (15-ounce) can fire-roasted crushed or diced tomatoes
✹ 2 cups vegetable broth
✹ 1 cup medium-spicy chipotle salsa
✹ 1 (10-ounce) bag frozen corn

1. With the pressure cooker on the brown or sauté setting, heat the vegetable oil until it shimmers. As the oil is heating, cut 4 of the tortillas in half, then cut each half into ½-inch wide strips. Working in batches if necessary, fry the tortilla strips in the oil, using tongs or a spatula to turn them over so they cook on both sides. When crisp, remove the tortillas from the pot and drain on a paper towel-covered plate or baking sheet. Immediately sprinkle them with 1 teaspoon of kosher salt. Set aside. Drain any excess oil out of the pressure cooker pot.

2. Roughly tear the remaining 2 tortillas into large pieces and place them in a blender with the tomatoes and remaining salt. Pulse until the tortilla is puréed. Add this tomato mixture, the broth, and the salsa to the pressure cooker pot.

3. Lock on the lid and set the timer for 10 minutes at high pressure. When the timer goes off, natural release the pressure. Remove the lid and stir in the corn.

4. Lock on the lid and set the timer for 2 minutes at high pressure. When the timer goes off, quick release the pressure, remove the lid, and stir. Ladle a serving of hot soup into each bowl and garnish each with a handful of fried tortilla strips.

Butternut Squash Soup with Coconut and Ginger

PREP TIME: 15 MINUTES • COOK TIME: 15 MINUTES AT HIGH PRESSURE, QUICK RELEASE

SERVES 4 TO 6 Ginger and coconut milk give this squash soup an exotic twist. Because of the naturally sweet flavor of the squash and the smooth consistency of the soup, this is a particularly popular meal among kids. Mine enjoy it with garlic bread and a side salad. I keep a jar of prepared minced ginger on hand for recipes, like this one, that call for fresh ginger—it saves the time of peeling and grating a knob of the root.

GLUTEN-FREE
SOY-FREE
NUT-FREE
VEGAN

- 1 tablespoon extra-virgin olive oil
- ❋ 1 small yellow onion, diced
- ❋ 1 butternut squash, peeled and cut into chunks
- ❋ 4 cups vegetable stock
- ❋ 1 cup coconut milk
- ❋ 2 teaspoons minced fresh ginger
- ¼ teaspoon kosher salt
- ⅛ teaspoon freshly ground black pepper
- ⅛ teaspoon ground nutmeg

1. With the pressure cooker on the brown or sauté setting, heat the olive oil until it shimmers. Add the onion and sauté, stirring frequently, until it is softened and translucent, about 5 minutes. Add the squash, vegetable stock, coconut milk, ginger, salt, pepper, and nutmeg. Stir to combine.

2. Lock on the lid and set the timer for 15 minutes at high pressure. When the timer goes off, quick release the pressure and remove the lid.

3. Use an immersion blender to purée the soup, or let it cool slightly and transfer it to a blender to purée, making sure to vent the lid so steam can escape.

Cheesy Cauliflower Soup

PREP TIME: 10 MINUTES • COOK TIME: 10 MINUTES AT HIGH PRESSURE, QUICK RELEASE

SERVES 4 Cauliflower is one of those versatile ingredients that can easily take on flavors of other, less healthy ingredients: in this case, cheese. This soup tastes far richer than it actually is. Because Gruyère and Emmental cheese are the same cheeses used in fondue, I've echoed that theme with a splash of white wine, another common ingredient in the famous Swiss dish. If you don't want to use wine, a tablespoon of apple cider vinegar would work in its place.

1. With the pressure cooker on the brown or sauté setting, heat the olive oil until it shimmers. Add the mirepoix and sauté, stirring frequently, until the onion is softened and translucent, about 5 minutes. Add the cauliflower, broth, and bay leaf; stir to combine.

2. Lock on the lid and set the timer for 10 minutes at high pressure. When the timer goes off, quick release the pressure. Open the lid and remove and discard the bay leaf.

3. Use an immersion blender to purée the soup or let it cool slightly and transfer it to a blender to purée, making sure to vent the lid so steam can escape. Stir in the cheese and white wine, and add the salt and pepper.

SOY-FREE
NUT-FREE

3 tablespoons unsalted butter

☀ 1 cup mirepoix-style vegetable blend (diced onion, celery, and carrot)

☀ 1 cauliflower head, chopped into florets

☀ 4 cups vegetable broth or vegetarian chicken-flavored broth

1 bay leaf

☀ 1 cup grated Gruyère or Emmental cheese

☀ ⅛ cup dry white wine

¼ teaspoon kosher salt

⅛ teaspoon freshly ground white pepper

Serving Tip *A nice garnish for this soup is a cheese crouton: toast a small slice of baguette for each serving, top it with grated cheese, and broil it until the cheese melts and bubbles. Float the crouton on each bowl of soup.*

Rosemary Potato-Leek Soup

PREP TIME: 10 MINUTES • COOK TIME: 5 MINUTES AT HIGH PRESSURE, NATURAL RELEASE

SERVES 6 This classic potato soup gets a fresh kick from woodsy rosemary, which gives it a flavor that's just right for late fall or winter. Replacing the rosemary with fresh dill changes the flavor profile, making it more appropriate for spring or summer. And adding chives, plus a sprinkling of grated Cheddar cheese and a dollop of sour cream as a garnish, turns it into baked potato soup. In other words, it's a wonderfully versatile recipe, so feel free to play with it.

1. With the pressure cooker on the brown or sauté setting, heat the butter until it melts. Add the leeks and sauté, stirring frequently, until they are softened and translucent, about 5 minutes. Add the potatoes, 2 tablespoons of rosemary, and stock.

2. Lock on the lid and set the timer for 5 minutes at high pressure. When the timer goes off, natural release the pressure for 10 minutes, then quick release any remaining pressure.

3. Use an immersion blender to purée the soup or let it cool slightly and transfer it to a blender to purée, making sure to vent the lid so steam can escape. Stir in the cream and add the salt and pepper. Serve hot, garnished with the remaining 1 teaspoon of rosemary.

GLUTEN-FREE
SOY-FREE
NUT-FREE

2 tablespoons unsalted butter

* 2 leeks, white part only, diced
* 2 pounds white potatoes, such as russets, peeled and cut into 1-inch cubes
* 2 tablespoons minced fresh rosemary, plus 1 teaspoon, divided
* 3 cups vegetarian chicken-flavored stock
* ½ cup heavy (whipping) cream

½ teaspoon kosher salt

¼ teaspoon ground white pepper

Ingredient Tip *Russet potatoes are ideal for a puréed soup because they have a mealy, starchy texture that breaks down easily.*

Black Bean Soup with Chard and Veggie Sausage

PREP TIME: 15 MINUTES • COOK TIME: 43 MINUTES AT HIGH PRESSURE, NATURAL RELEASE

SERVES 4 TO 6 A handful of flavorful meatless sausage chunks lends a heartier flavor to this black bean soup, while chard adds texture and ramps up the health quotient. Look for boldly flavored veggie sausages, such as spicy Italian- or Andouille-style versions. If you want to go sausage-free, I recommend stirring in a bag of frozen corn or a can of diced tomatoes and green chiles (such as Ro-Tel) during the 3-minute cooking period at the end. I like to serve this with a dollop of sour cream or guacamole.

NUT-FREE
VEGAN

1 tablespoon extra-virgin olive oil

❋ 1 large onion, diced

❋ 1 pound dried black beans, rinsed

❋ 6 cups low-sodium vegetable broth

1 bay leaf

½ teaspoon garlic powder

1 teaspoon chipotle seasoning

1 teaspoon kosher salt

¼ teaspoon freshly ground black pepper

❋ 1 chard bunch, stemmed, rinsed well, and chopped (about 3 cups)

❋ 4 vegetarian spicy sausage links, cut into ½-inch rounds

1. With the pressure cooker on the brown or sauté setting, heat the olive oil until it shimmers. Add the onion and sauté, stirring frequently, until it is softened and translucent, about 5 minutes. Stir in the beans, vegetable broth, bay leaf, garlic powder, chipotle seasoning, salt, and pepper.

2. Lock on the lid and set the timer for 40 minutes at high pressure. When the timer goes off, natural release the pressure for 10 minutes. Quick release any remaining pressure, then remove the lid.

3. Scoop out about a cup of beans into a medium bowl. Use a wooden spoon or a bean masher to mash the beans until they're a rough purée. Stir them back into the pot, along with the chard and sausage.

4. Lock the lid back on and set the timer for 3 minutes at high pressure. When the timer goes off, quick release the pressure, remove the lid, and stir the soup before serving.

Lentil-Mushroom Stew

PREP TIME: 15 MINUTES • COOK TIME: 10 MINUTES AT HIGH PRESSURE, NATURAL RELEASE

SERVES 6 This hearty stew is chock-full of vegetables, lentils, and meaty mushrooms. It's great on its own, but top it with the fluffy Dumplings (page 140) to make it even more substantial. Cremini mushrooms are used here, but you can use any type of mushroom that you like. Be sure to use brown lentils, which hold their shape better than the red ones.

GLUTEN-FREE
NUT-FREE

1 tablespoon extra-virgin olive oil

☀ 1 medium yellow onion, diced

☀ 2 carrots, peeled and sliced into ½-inch pieces

☀ 8 ounces cremini mushrooms, quartered

☀ 1½ cups brown lentils

☀ 4 cups vegetable broth

½ teaspoon dried thyme

1 cup water

¼ teaspoon kosher salt

⅛ teaspoon freshly ground black pepper

1. With the pressure cooker on the brown or sauté setting, heat the olive oil until it shimmers. Add the onion and sauté, stirring frequently, until it is softened and translucent, about 5 minutes. Add the carrots, mushrooms, lentils, vegetable broth, thyme, and water. Stir to combine, making sure to scrape down any stray bits of lentil or vegetables from the side of the pot.

2. Lock on the lid and set the timer for 10 minutes at high pressure. When the timer goes off, natural release the pressure for 10 minutes. Quick release any remaining pressure, and remove the lid. Add the salt and pepper and stir to combine.

Corn Chowder

PREP TIME: 15 MINUTES • COOK TIME: 11 MINUTES AT HIGH PRESSURE, QUICK RELEASE

SERVES 6 TO 8 I recently learned from a recipe on the stellar cooking website Serious Eats that simmering corncobs in the cooking liquid intensifies the corn flavor, and adds starch to the mixture that gives it a natural thickness and body. This is a recipe I love to make in the summertime, when you can buy five ears of fresh corn for a dollar at the supermarket or at the farmers' market. You can use frozen corn on the cob in a pinch.

1. With the pressure cooker on the brown or sauté setting, melt the butter until it foams. Add the mirepoix and sauté, stirring frequently, until the vegetables are softened and the onion is translucent, 5 to 7 minutes. Place the corn kernels in the pressure cooker pot. Add the water, bay leaf, thyme, and bacon salt.

2. Lock on the lid and set the timer for 8 minutes at high pressure. When the timer goes off, quick release the pressure. Remove the lid and add the potatoes and the corncobs, stirring to make sure they are submerged in the liquid.

3. Lock on the lid and set the timer for 3 minutes at high pressure. When the timer goes off, quick release the pressure again and remove the lid. Remove and discard the corncobs and the bay leaf.

4. Stir the evaporated milk into the chowder and add the salt and pepper. Serve hot.

GLUTEN-FREE
NUT-FREE

2 tablespoons unsalted butter

☀ 1 cup mirepoix-style vegetable blend (diced onion, carrots, and celery)

☀ 4 to 5 sweet corn ears, kernels removed, cut in quarters, cobs reserved

3 cups water

1 bay leaf

½ teaspoon dried thyme

½ teaspoon bacon salt

☀ 2 medium Yukon gold potatoes, peeled and cut into 1-inch cubes

☀ 1 cup evaporated milk

¼ teaspoon kosher salt

¼ teaspoon freshly ground black pepper

Ingredient Tip *Whereas russet potatoes are best for a recipe where the potatoes will be mashed or puréed, I like using Yukon golds in a recipe where you want the potatoes to retain their shape.*

French Onion Soup

PREP TIME: 15 MINUTES • COOK TIME: 20 MINUTES AT HIGH PRESSURE, QUICK RELEASE

SERVES 6 A mainstay at French brasseries, French Onion Soup is usually made with beef stock. I've found that mushroom stock or broth is a flavorful substitute for giving that umami flavor that makes this soup so complex, as does a dash of soy sauce. Starting with already sweet Vidalia onions helps replicate the caramelized flavor that's usually achieved by a long simmer on the stove. And don't forget the best part: a generous cap of melting cheese!

NUT-FREE

- 4 tablespoons unsalted butter
- ✴ 4 large Vidalia onions, thinly sliced
- 2 tablespoons brown sugar
- ½ teaspoon baking soda
- ✴ 6 cups mushroom stock, divided
- 2 tablespoons apple cider vinegar
- 1 bay leaf
- ✴ 1 teaspoon soy sauce
- ✴ 6 slices French bread, toasted
- ✴ 1½ cups grated Gruyère cheese

Preparation Tip *To make cutting the onions easier, use a mandoline slicer. This kitchen tool speeds the slicing of any type of fruit or vegetable, making thin, even slices quickly.*

1. With the pressure cooker on the brown or sauté setting, melt the butter until it foams. Add the onions and sauté, stirring frequently, until softened and translucent, 5 to 7 minutes. Sprinkle the brown sugar and baking soda over the onions. Stir in ½ cup mushroom stock.

2. Lock on the lid and set the timer for 20 minutes at high pressure. If the pressure cooker doesn't come up to pressure, it means there's not enough liquid. Add another ½ cup of stock and reset the timer. When the timer goes off, quick release the pressure. Remove the lid and turn the pressure cooker back to the sauté setting.

3. Cook the onions, stirring frequently, until the liquid cooks off and the onions are browned and syrupy. Add the vinegar to the pot and stir, scraping any browned bits off the bottom of the pot. Pour in the remaining 5½ cups mushroom stock, and add the bay leaf and soy sauce.

4. Lock on the lid and set the timer for 5 minutes at high pressure. When the timer goes off, quick release the pressure.

5. Ladle soup into a bowl. Top each bowl with a piece of toasted bread and about ¼ cup of grated cheese. If desired, place the bowl under a broiler until the cheese melts and bubbles. If you choose to do this, make sure the bowls you use are ovenproof.

Hoppin' John

PREP TIME: 15 MINUTES • COOK TIME: 8 MINUTES, AT HIGH PRESSURE, NATURAL RELEASE

SERVES 4 TO 6 As a Southerner (at least for the past decade), I'd be remiss in not including one of my favorite regional dishes. Hoppin' John is the name given to a stew made of black-eyed peas and is traditionally eaten on New Year's Day. It's said that you get a day of good luck for every black-eyed pea you eat, and this legend hasn't let me down yet. Spoon it over Basic White Rice (page 25) with a side of Stewed Collard Greens (page 57), like most of my neighbors here do.

GLUTEN-FREE

SOY-FREE

NUT-FREE

VEGAN

1 tablespoon vegetable oil

✳ 1 medium yellow onion, diced

✳ 1 celery rib, diced

✳ 1 medium red bell pepper, seeded and diced

✳ 1 pound dried black-eyed peas, rinsed

✳ 4 cups vegetable stock

1 teaspoon garlic powder

1 teaspoon bacon salt

⅛ teaspoon ground cayenne pepper

1 bay leaf

½ teaspoon kosher salt

⅛ teaspoon freshly ground black pepper

1. With the pressure cooker on the brown or sauté setting, heat the vegetable oil until it shimmers. Add the onion, celery, and bell pepper and sauté, stirring frequently, until they soften and become translucent, 5 to 7 minutes. Add the peas, vegetable stock, garlic powder, bacon salt, cayenne pepper, and bay leaf.

2. Lock on the lid and set the timer for 8 minutes at high pressure. When the timer goes off, natural release the pressure for 10 minutes. Quick release any remaining pressure and remove the lid. Stir the stew, remove and discard the bay leaf, and add the salt and pepper.

Classic Chili

PREP TIME: 15 MINUTES • COOK TIME: 7 MINUTES AT HIGH PRESSURE, NATURAL RELEASE

SERVES 4 TO 6 This chili recipe is in weekly rotation in my household; it's one of those recipes that is easy to put together because I always have the ingredients in the pantry and freezer. You can add meatless crumbles to it for a more traditional texture, but I find that it's still hearty without them. Serve it with your favorite toppings, such as sour cream or plain Greek yogurt, grated Colby cheese, black olives, or chopped scallions.

GLUTEN-FREE
SOY-FREE
NUT-FREE
VEGAN

- 1 tablespoon vegetable oil
- ✳ 1 medium yellow onion, diced
- ✳ 1 (28-ounce) can crushed tomatoes, preferably fire-roasted
- ✳ 2 tablespoons tomato paste
- ✳ 2 (15-ounce) cans kidney beans, drained and rinsed
- ✳ 1 (10-ounce) bag frozen corn kernels
- 1 tablespoon ground cumin
- 1 teaspoon chili powder
- 1 teaspoon dried oregano
- 1 teaspoon kosher salt
- ¼ teaspoon freshly ground black pepper

1. With the pressure cooker on the brown or sauté setting, heat the vegetable oil until it shimmers. Add the onion and sauté, stirring frequently, until it is softened and translucent, about 5 minutes. Stir in the crushed tomatoes, tomato paste, beans, frozen corn, cumin, chili powder, oregano, salt, and pepper.

2. Lock on the lid and set the timer for 7 minutes at high pressure. When the timer goes off, natural release the pressure for 5 minutes, then quick release any remaining pressure. Remove the lid and stir the chili. Serve hot.

Ingredient Tip *Small as the cans are, it's rare that you need an entire can of tomato paste in a recipe. I like to portion the rest of the tomato paste in tablespoon-size dollops onto a length of parchment paper, freeze them, then transfer the frozen dollops into a zip-top freezer bag for the next time I need a tablespoon or two. If you're using it in a cooked sauce or a stew, you don't even need to thaw it first!*

Quick Quinoa Chili

PREP TIME: 5 MINUTES • COOK TIME: 4 MINUTES AT HIGH PRESSURE, NATURAL RELEASE

SERVES 4 TO 6 With its high protein content but neutral flavor, quinoa is a good substitute for meat in this recipe, particularly if you don't eat soy-based meat replacements. No chopping is needed for this chili, so it's a good meal to throw together in a hurry. Of course, it's not complete without a dollop of sour cream or plain Greek yogurt on top and a sprinkle of scallions. My family likes when I heat the leftovers and serve them over spaghetti.

GLUTEN-FREE
SOY-FREE
NUT-FREE
VEGAN

* 1 (28-ounce) can diced tomatoes with green pepper, celery, and onion, undrained
* 2 (15-ounce) cans kidney beans, drained and rinsed
* ½ cup white quinoa
* 2 cups frozen corn
* 1 cup vegetable broth
  1 tablespoon ground cumin
  1 teaspoon chili powder
  1 teaspoon kosher salt
  ½ teaspoon garlic powder

1. In the pressure cooker pot, combine the tomatoes, beans, quinoa, corn, broth, cumin, chili powder, salt, and garlic powder. Stir to combine the ingredients well.

2. Lock on the lid and set the timer for 4 minutes at high pressure. When the timer goes off, let the pressure natural release for 5 minutes, then quick release any remaining pressure. Stir the chili. If it is still very watery, replace the lid and let the chili sit for a few minutes so the quinoa can absorb more of the liquid. Serve hot, garnished with your favorite chili toppings.

White Bean Chili

PREP TIME: 15 MINUTES ● COOK TIME: 25 MINUTES AT HIGH PRESSURE, NATURAL RELEASE

SERVES 4 TO 6 This hearty dish is an unexpected variation on traditional chili. It is made with white beans and flavored with salsa verde (green salsa) instead of a tomato-based variety. As a result, it's soupier than traditional chili. You can thicken it by scooping out a cup or so of the cooked beans, mashing them well with the back of a spoon, and stirring them back into the pot. This chili is especially delicious topped with crumbled queso fresco, diced avocado, and a dollop of sour cream. Serve it with Cheesy Cornbread (page 141) or some warm tortillas.

1. With the pressure cooker on the sauté or brown setting, heat the oil. Add the onion and sauté it, stirring occasionally, until it is soft, about 5 minutes. Add the beans, broth, cumin, and garlic powder. Stir to combine.

2. Lock on the lid and set the timer to cook on high for 25 minutes at high pressure. When the timer goes off, turn off or unplug the cooker and natural release the pressure for 15 minutes, then quick release the remaining pressure in short spurts until all has been released.

3. Stir in the salsa verde and meatless crumbles. Replace the lid and let the chili sit for 5 minutes to heat the crumbles through. Serve hot.

NUT-FREE

1 tablespoon vegetable oil
1 cup diced white onion
1 pound dried great northern beans, rinsed, unsoaked
3 cups vegetarian chicken-flavored broth
2 teaspoons ground cumin
½ teaspoon garlic powder
¾ cup salsa verde
1 cup meatless chicken-style crumbles

Ingredient Tip *As a variation, try using frozen corn instead of or in addition to the meatless crumbles.*

Chapter Four

EXTRAS

DESSERTS

121

SAUCES AND MORE

135

DESSERTS

122   Berry Cobbler

123   Red Wine Poached Pears

124   Stuffed Apples

125   Honey Stewed Figs with Goat Cheese

126   Lemon-Ricotta Cups

127   Orange Crème Brûlée

128   Two-Layer Cheesecake

130   Cardamom Rice Pudding

131   Pumpkin Bread Pudding

132   Brownie Pudding Cake

133   Lemon Curd

Berry Cobbler

PREP TIME: 10 MINUTES • COOK TIME: 23 MINUTES AT HIGH PRESSURE, QUICK RELEASE

SERVES 4 I keep bags of frozen fruit on hand so that I can throw together this quick, comforting dessert at a moment's notice. I particularly love when I have black-berries or blueberries frozen from the summer's harvest. Frozen fruit, because it's already broken down a bit, works well to make a super-syrupy cobbler filling. Serve this with a scoop of vanilla ice cream or a dollop of whipped cream.

1. Place the berries in a 1-quart heat-proof, tempered baking dish. Sprinkle them with the sugar and cornstarch and stir to combine.

2. In a small bowl, combine the rolled oats, brown sugar, butter, and flour. Use a fork to mash the butter into the dry ingredients, working it in until the butter is fully integrated with the other ingredients, making a crumbly mixture. Sprinkle this mixture evenly over the berries.

3. Place the rack into the pressure cooker pot. Pour the water into the pot and place the baking dish on the rack. Lock on the lid and set the timer for 23 minutes. When the timer goes off, quick release the pressure. Care-fully remove the baking dish from the pressure cooker and allow the cobbler to cool slightly. Serve warm or at room temperature.

SOY-FREE

NUT-FREE

* 12 ounces frozen berries, such as blueberries, blackberries, raspberries, or a combination, thawed
1 tablespoon granulated sugar
1½ teaspoons cornstarch
* ¼ cup rolled oats
2 tablespoons brown sugar
2 tablespoons unsalted butter, at room temperature
1 tablespoon all-purpose flour
1 cup water

Serving Tip *If you want the topping to have a bit more crunch, stir a couple of tablespoons of sliced, toasted almonds or chopped pecans into the oat topping.*

Red Wine Poached Pears

PREP TIME: 10 MINUTES • COOK TIME: 4 MINUTES AT HIGH PRESSURE, QUICK RELEASE

SERVES 4 This elegant dessert is particularly nice in the autumn, when pears are in season. The pears can be served chilled or warm, perhaps with ice cream, vanilla yogurt, or mascarpone spooned on top. They're also delicious as a topping for Cardamom Rice Pudding (page 130). Look for firm pears like Anjou or Bartlett. The real vanilla bean adds a lot of flavor to the poaching liquid, but if you don't have one, you can add ½ teaspoon of vanilla extract at the very end of cooking.

GLUTEN-FREE

SOY-FREE

NUT-FREE

VEGAN

* 3 cups fruity red wine, such as zinfandel
* ¼ cup granulated sugar
* ½ cup freshly squeezed orange juice
* ½ teaspoon ground cinnamon
* 1 vanilla bean, split
* 2 whole cloves
* 4 pears, peeled, halved, and cored

1. Pour the wine into the pressure cooker pot. Add the sugar, orange juice, cinnamon, vanilla bean, and cloves. Stir to combine and to dissolve the sugar. Place the pears in the poaching liquid and spoon some of the liquid over the top of the fruit.

2. Lock on the lid and set the timer for 4 minutes at high pressure. When the timer goes off, quick release the pressure and remove the lid. With tongs, remove the pears and put them on a platter.

3. Turn the pressure cooker to brown or sauté (or the simmer setting, if yours has one) and simmer the sauce until it is reduced by half and syrupy, about 10 minutes. Spoon the sauce over the pears and serve.

Preparation Tip *To prepare the pears, use a vegetable peeler or a paring knife to peel the skin. Cut the pears in half lengthwise. Use a spoon to scoop out the core with the seeds.*

Stuffed Apples

PREP TIME: 5 MINUTES • COOK TIME: 8 MINUTES AT HIGH PRESSURE, NATURAL RELEASE

SERVES 4 Autumn, when apples are fresh off the tree, is the best time to make this recipe. I recommend using a firm apple, such as a Granny Smith or a Pink Lady, so that it holds its shape better. These apples make a healthy dessert, served warm in a bowl with some of the cooking liquid spooned over them. Of course, you can add some whipped cream, a splash of heavy cream, or a scoop of ice cream, too.

GLUTEN-FREE

SOY-FREE

NUT-FREE

- ½ cup rolled oats
  2 tablespoons brown sugar
- ¼ cup raisins
  1 teaspoon ground cinnamon
  3 tablespoons unsalted butter, at room temperature, divided
- 4 apples, cored, peels intact
- 1½ cups apple cider

1. In a small bowl, combine the oats, sugar, raisins, and cinnamon. Using a fork, work 2 tablespoons of butter into the mixture, mashing the butter until it is well blended into the dry ingredients.

2. Place the apples in the pressure cooker pot and fill the cavities of each apple with the oat mixture, packing it in as tightly as possible. Any remaining mixture can be sprinkled over the apples. Pour the cider into the pot around the apples. Dot the remaining 1 tablespoon of butter over the apples.

3. Lock on the lid and set the timer for 8 minutes at high pressure. When the timer goes off, natural release the pressure completely and open the lid. Use a spoon scooped completely under the apples to remove each, so the filling doesn't fall out. Serve the apples in bowls, with the cooking liquid spooned over, if desired.

Honey Stewed Figs with Goat Cheese

PREP TIME: 5 MINUTES • COOK TIME: 5 MINUTES AT HIGH PRESSURE, QUICK RELEASE

SERVES 4 TO 6 This sophisticated dessert is great for a dinner party, served with the rest of the bottle of wine used as the poaching liquid. These figs are great served warm as they are prepared here, or try them spooned over a slice of pound cake. The most common dried figs you'll find are Turkish figs or Mission figs. Mission figs, which are dark and teardrop-shaped, are probably easier to find, but I think Turkish figs look prettier.

1. In the pressure cooker pot, combine the wine, ¼ cup of honey, cinnamon, cloves, and star anise. Stir to combine and to dissolve the honey. Place the figs in the pot.

2. Lock on the lid and set the timer for 5 minutes at high pressure. When the timer goes off, quick release the pressure. Spoon the figs into a serving dish and crumble the goat cheese over them. Drizzle them with the remaining 1 tablespoon of honey. Serves warm.

GLUTEN-FREE
SOY-FREE
NUT-FREE

* 1½ cups sweet white wine, at room temperature
* ¼ cup honey, plus 1 tablespoon, divided
* 1 teaspoon ground cinnamon
* ½ teaspoon ground cloves
* 1 whole star anise
* 12 dried figs, halved lengthwise
* 4 ounces goat cheese, crumbled

Ingredient Tip *Any type of sweet wine or port can be used. Good options include Riesling, Moscato, or Sauternes. If you don't drink wine, use apple juice or cider instead.*

Lemon-Ricotta Cups

PREP TIME: 15 MINUTES • COOK TIME: 15 MINUTES AT HIGH PRESSURE, NATURAL RELEASE

SERVES 6 These delicately flavored treats are a cross between a pudding and a cake. I like eating them warm, right out of the cups, but if you grease them enough with butter, you can unmold them, upside down, onto a plate and spoon some Quick Berry Compote (page 143) on top for a show-stopping dessert. You could also spoon some jam or compote (raspberry would complement the lemon) into the bottom of the cup before adding the batter.

SOY-FREE
NUT-FREE

1 cup water
½ cup (1 stick) unsalted butter, plus 1 tablespoon, at room temperature
1 cup granulated sugar
✳ 4 ounces (about ½ cup) ricotta cheese
✳ 2 eggs, lightly beaten
✳ Zest of 1 lemon
✳ Juice of 2 lemons
✳ 1 cup all-purpose flour
1 teaspoon baking powder
¼ teaspoon kosher salt

1. Place the rack in the pressure cooker pot. Add the water to the pot. Use 1 tablespoon of butter to generously grease the insides of 6 (1-cup) ramekins or custard cups. Set aside.

2. In a large bowl, with a fork or a hand mixer, mix together the remaining 4 ounces of butter, sugar, and ricotta cheese until smooth. Stir in the eggs followed by the lemon zest. Stir in the lemon juice.

3. In a small bowl, whisk together the flour, baking powder, and salt. Stir these dry ingredients into the batter just until combined.

4. Divide the batter evenly between the prepared ramekins, filling each about halfway. Tightly cover each ramekin with aluminum foil. Arrange the ramekins on the rack in the pressure cooker, stacking them if necessary. You can use another rack or a heat-proof trivet on top of the first layer of ramekins so that the second layer will sit level.

5. Lock on the lid and set the timer for 15 minutes at high pressure. When the timer goes off, natural release the pressure for 10 minutes. Quick release any remaining pressure, open the lid, and use tongs to remove the ramekins. Uncover and serve warm or at room temperature.

Orange Crème Brûlée

PREP TIME: 10 MINUTES • COOK TIME: 8 MINUTES AT LOW PRESSURE, NATURAL RELEASE

SERVES 4 Crème brûlée done right is a delicious contrast of creamy and crisp, cool and warm. I love to order it in restaurants, but the truth is, it's not hard to make at home. Make the custards ahead of time and chill them well, then torch (or broil) the sugar just before serving. The idea is that your spoon will crack the brittle shell of sugar to scoop out a bite of custard that's cool on the bottom but still warm on the top.

GLUTEN-FREE
SOY-FREE
NUT-FREE

2 cups water

✳ 6 egg yolks

⅓ cup granulated sugar

✳ 1½ cups heavy
   (whipping) cream

✳ 2 teaspoons orange extract

1 teaspoon vanilla extract

✳ 4 tablespoons
   superfine sugar

Cooking Tip *If you don't have a culinary torch, preheat your broiler. Place the chilled custards on a baking sheet, sprinkle the tops with the superfine sugar, and broil them for 2 to 3 minutes or until the sugar bubbles and caramelizes.*

1. Place the rack in the pressure cooker pot and add the water to the pot.

2. In a large mixing bowl, add the egg yolks and granulated sugar and whisk until smooth. Gradually whisk in the heavy cream, orange extract, and vanilla extract. Pour the mixture into four heat-proof ramekins or custard cups. Cover each tightly with aluminum foil, and arrange the ramekins on the rack in the pressure cooker, stacking them if needed.

3. Lock on the lid and set the timer for 8 minutes at low pressure. When the timer goes off, natural release the pressure for 10 minutes, then quick release any remaining pressure. Check the custards: they should be just set, but still jiggly in the middle. If liquid remains in the ramekins, pressure cook for 1 to 2 minutes more.

4. When the custards are done, remove the foil and cool on a wire rack for 30 to 45 minutes until they reach room temperature. Then cover each tightly with plastic wrap and refrigerate until chilled, at least 2 hours.

5. Just before serving, sprinkle each custard evenly with the superfine sugar. Use a culinary torch to broil the sugar until it bubbles and caramelizes. Let them sit for a moment until the sugar hardens. Serve immediately.

Two-Layer Cheesecake

PREP TIME: 15 MINUTES • COOK TIME: 18 MINUTES AT LOW PRESSURE, NATURAL RELEASE

SERVES 8 This cheesecake is based on the recipe my mom prepared when I was a kid. I loved its two layers: a dense, sweet, and creamy bottom layer topped with a lighter layer of tangy sour cream. In the pressure cooker, the bottom layer gets an airy texture that's almost like a soufflé. Don't worry if it seems like there won't be room to spread the sour cream layer—once it you start spooning it on top, the cake will deflate a bit under its weight.

SOY-FREE
NUT-FREE

* ½ cup graham cracker crumbs
* 1 tablespoon unsalted butter, melted
* ¾ cup granulated sugar, divided
* 12 ounces cream cheese, at room temperature
* 1½ teaspoons vanilla extract, divided
* 2 eggs, room temperature
* 1¼ cups sour cream, divided
* 1 cup water

Ingredient Tip *Be sure that all of your ingredients, particularly the eggs and cream cheese, are at room temperature when you start. Otherwise the mixture will be lumpy.*

1. In a small bowl, combine the graham cracker crumbs, melted butter, and 2 tablespoons granulated sugar until it resembles damp sand. Press the mixture evenly into the bottom and about ½ inch up the sides of a 7-inch spring-form pan. Place in the freezer for at least 20 minutes to firm up, or until needed.

2. Place the cream cheese in a large bowl and combine it with ½ of cup sugar. With a hand mixer, blend the cream cheese with the sugar until it is smooth and creamy. Add the eggs, one at a time, blending well between additions. Add ¼ cup of sour cream and 1 teaspoon vanilla and blend well. Pour the mixture into the springform pan.

3. Place a rack in the pot of a pressure cooker with the lifting handles turned up (or you can fold an 18-inch piece of aluminum foil into a sling to put under the pan so it can be lifted out easily). Add the water to the cooker and carefully lower the pan onto the rack, using the sling if helpful. Lock on the lid and set the timer for 15 minutes at low pressure.

4. While the cheesecake is cooking, in a small bowl, mix together the remaining 1 cup of sour cream, 2 tablespoons of sugar, and ½ teaspoon of vanilla. Set aside.

5. When the timer goes off, natural release the pressure for 10 minutes, then quick release any remaining pressure and remove the lid. Carefully take the cake out of the cooker, spread the sour cream mixture over the cake, and return it to the rack in the cooker. Lock the lid into place and set the timer for 3 minutes at low pressure. When the timer goes off, natural release the pressure for 10 minutes as before.

6. Let the cheesecake cool on a cooling rack until lukewarm to the touch, then transfer to the refrigerator and refrigerate for several hours, until firm.

Cardamom Rice Pudding

PREP TIME: 10 MINUTES • COOK TIME: 10 MINUTES AT LOW PRESSURE, NATURAL RELEASE

SERVES 4 Rice pudding always takes me back to my childhood. My mom used to make it when I was not feeling well. Although she insisted on chilling it before we ate it, I have since found that it's absolutely fantastic served warm from the pot, perhaps with a dollop of whipped cream or a splash of milk. Cinnamon is the typical flavoring, but I like the exotic flavor of cardamom, a ginger-related spice from Southeast Asia.

GLUTEN-FREE

SOY-FREE

NUT-FREE

* 3 cups whole milk
  ⅓ cup granulated sugar
* ½ teaspoon
  ground cardamom
* 1 cup Arborio rice
  ⅛ teaspoon kosher salt
* 2 eggs
  1 teaspoon vanilla extract

Preparation Tip *Gradually warming up the eggs by adding in some of the hot rice mixture helps prevent the eggs from scrambling when poured into the pot. This process is called tempering.*

1. With the pressure cooker on the sauté or brown setting, combine the milk, sugar, and cardamom. Heat it until the sugar is dissolved. Stir in the rice and salt.

2. Lock on the lid and set the timer for 10 minutes at low pressure. When the timer goes off, turn off or unplug the pressure cooker and natural release the pressure for 10 minutes. Quick release the remaining pressure and open the lid.

3. In a small bowl, whisk the eggs. Spoon some of the cooked rice mixture (it should be a little soupy) into the bowl with the eggs and stir to combine with the whisk or a spoon. Gradually stir in more of the rice mixture until the egg mixture is very warm. Pour the egg mixture into the pot and stir to combine.

4. Turn the pressure cooker to the sauté or brown setting and cook for 2 to 3 minutes, until the mixture has thickened like a custard sauce. Stir in the vanilla extract. Serve warm, or transfer to individual bowls and chill. The pudding will thicken further as it cools.

Pumpkin Bread Pudding

PREP TIME: 15 MINUTES • COOK TIME: 20 MINUTES AT LOW PRESSURE, NATURAL RELEASE

SERVES 4 This deliciously spiced dessert is a great option for Thanksgiving or any fall dinner. Use a rich, eggy bread like challah or brioche; like the French Toast Casserole (page 82) or the Strata (page 81), the bread should be slightly stale so that it can absorb as much of the rich custard as possible. If you don't have pumpkin pie spice, use a combination of cinnamon, ground ginger, and cloves.

SOY-FREE
NUT-FREE

2 tablespoons unsalted butter, divided

❋ 1 small loaf challah or brioche bread, cut into cubes

❋ ½ cup golden raisins

❋ 3 eggs

❋ 1 cup whole milk

❋ ½ cup pumpkin purée

¼ cup granulated sugar

1 tablespoon vanilla extract

1½ teaspoons pumpkin pie spice

⅛ teaspoon kosher salt

1 cup water

1. In a 2-quart tempered glass baking dish that fits into the pot of your pressure cooker, rub the bottom and insides with 1 tablespoon of butter. Pile the bread cubes in the dish, toss with the raisins, and set aside.

2. In a large mixing bowl, whisk the eggs. Whisk in the milk, pumpkin purée, sugar, vanilla, pumpkin pie spice, and salt. Pour the mixture over the bread and use a wooden spoon or spatula to press the bread down to soak it completely with the custard. Let it sit for 5 minutes to allow the bread to absorb the custard.

3. Place the rack inside the pressure cooker pot and pour the water into the pot. Cut the remaining 1 tablespoon of butter into small pieces and dot them over the bread. Cover the baking dish with aluminum foil and place the dish on the rack.

4. Lock on the lid and set the timer for 20 minutes at low pressure. When the timer goes off, natural release the pressure for 10 minutes. Quick release any remaining pressure and carefully take the baking dish out of the pressure cooker. Serve hot.

Brownie Pudding Cake

PREP TIME: 10 MINUTES • COOK TIME: 18 MINUTES AT HIGH PRESSURE, QUICK RELEASE

SERVES 4 Remember when almost every restaurant had a chocolate lava cake on the dessert menu? For lovers of that rich chocolate dessert with the oozy middle, this brownie pudding cake is for you. I love the alchemy that happens in this recipe—the boiling water poured over the batter just before it goes into the cooker somehow transforms into that gooey filling. It's fantastic served with a dollop of whipped cream, a scoop of ice cream, or a splash of icy milk.

SOY-FREE
NUT-FREE

Unsalted butter
　for greasing, plus
　1 tablespoon melted
　then cooled
✳ ¼ cup plus 2 tablespoons
　all-purpose flour
¼ cup brown sugar, plus
　⅓ cup, divided
4 tablespoons cocoa
　powder, divided
1 teaspoon baking powder
¼ teaspoon kosher salt
✳ ¼ cup whole milk
½ teaspoon vanilla extract
¾ cup boiling water,
　plus 1 cup room
　temperature water

1. Butter a 1-quart heat-proof glass baking dish that is small enough to fit into your pressure cooker. Set aside.

2. In a medium mixing bowl, add the flour, ¼ cup of brown sugar, 2 tablespoons cocoa powder, baking powder, and salt. Stir with a whisk or a fork to combine. Stir in the milk, melted butter, and vanilla extract until a thick batter forms. Scrape the batter into the prepared baking dish.

3. In a small bowl, combine the remaining ⅓ cup of brown sugar and 2 tablespoons of cocoa powder. Sprinkle it evenly over the batter.

4. Place a rack in the pot of a pressure cooker with the lifting handles turned up (or you can fold an 18-inch piece of aluminum foil into a sling to put under the pan so it can be lifted out easily). Add 1 cup of water to the cooker. Pour ¾ cup boiling water over the batter and carefully lower the dish onto the rack, using the sling if helpful.

5. Lock on the lid and set the timer for 18 minutes at high pressure. When the timer goes off, quick release the pressure. Carefully take the cake out of the cooker, and let rest for 5 minutes before serving hot or warm.

Lemon Curd

PREP TIME: 10 MINUTES • COOK TIME: 12 MINUTES AT LOW PRESSURE, NATURAL RELEASE

MAKES 2 CUPS I'm surprised lemon curd isn't more popular and prevalent. Anyone who loves lemony desserts is sure to love its tart, creamy flavor, not to mention its versatility: swirl it into vanilla yogurt, slather it on toast or scones, use it between the layers of a cake, or spoon it into tart shells or onto tea cookies. It can be a challenge to make on the stove, since you have to watch carefully that the eggs don't curdle. But the pressure cooker eliminates all that fuss.

GLUTEN-FREE

SOY-FREE

NUT-FREE

4 tablespoons unsalted butter, at room temperature

1 cup sugar

✳ 2 large eggs

✳ 2 large egg yolks

✳ ½ cup freshly squeezed lemon juice

1 cup water

✳ Zest of 1 lemon

Cooking Tip *You can use this recipe to make grapefruit or lime curd; just substitute the other citrus juice for all or part of the lemon juice.*

1. In a 1-quart tempered glass bowl that fits in the pressure cooker, place the butter and sugar. Use the back of a spoon to mash the butter into the sugar until it's fully creamed.

2. In a small bowl, whisk together the eggs and the yolks. Add the eggs to the sugar mixture and stir to combine. Stir in the lemon juice. Cover the bowl tightly with aluminum foil.

3. Place the rack in the pressure cooker pot and add the water. Place the bowl of lemon curd on the rack. Lock on the lid and set the timer for 12 minutes at low pressure. When the timer goes off, natural release the pressure. Open the lid and carefully remove the bowl.

4. Remove the foil and stir in the zest with a whisk until the mixture is smooth. Let the curd cool to room temperature, then cover it tightly and refrigerate. The lemon curd will keep for up to 1 week.

SAUCES AND MORE

136 Herby Hummus

137 Hearty Tomato Sauce

138 Balsamic White Bean Dip

139 Garlicky Eggplant Dip

140 Dumplings for Stews and Soups

141 Cheesy Cornbread

142 Boiled Peanuts

143 Quick Berry Compote

144 Old-Fashioned Applesauce

145 Spiced Vanilla Caramel Sauce

146 Pumpkin Butter

Herby Hummus

PREP TIME: 15 MINUTES • COOK TIME: 45 MINUTES AT HIGH PRESSURE, NATURAL RELEASE

MAKES ABOUT 2 CUPS Homemade hummus is an entirely different world from store-bought versions. It has a denser, heartier texture, and the flavor of the chickpeas comes through much more strongly, especially when prepared from dried chickpeas. Use this hummus recipe as a base for your own, but feel free to play with additions. Kalamata olives or roasted red peppers would be tasty inclusions, as would a chipotle chile in adobo sauce.

GLUTEN-FREE

SOY-FREE

NUT-FREE

* ½ pound dried chickpeas
* 1½ teaspoons kosher salt, divided
* ½ cup low-fat plain yogurt
* 1 garlic clove, minced
* 2 tablespoons freshly squeezed lemon juice
* 2 teaspoons extra-virgin olive oil
* 1 tablespoon dried thyme
* 1 tablespoon dried dill
* 1 teaspoon ground cumin
* ⅛ teaspoon ground cayenne pepper

Serving Tip *Serve this hummus with home-made or store-bought pita chips, or as a dip for vegetables. It's also a good condiment slathered on a veggie sandwich.*

1. Place the chickpeas in the pressure cooker pot and add enough water (about 6 cups) to cover them by about 2 inches. Stir in ½ teaspoon of salt.

2. Lock on the lid and set the timer for 45 minutes at high pressure. When the timer goes off, natural release the pressure for 10 minutes, then quick release any remaining pressure. Drain the chickpeas in a colander and let them cool.

3. Transfer the chickpeas to the bowl of a food processor. Add the yogurt and garlic and process until creamy. Scrape down the sides of the bowl as needed to make sure everything gets well puréed. Add the lemon juice, olive oil, thyme, dill, cumin, cayenne pepper, and the remaining 1 teaspoon of salt, and pulse to mix. Continue to process until the mixture is smooth and creamy. It may take 2 or 3 minutes of processing to achieve the creamy texture. Transfer the hummus to a serving bowl and serve immediately or store, tightly covered and refrigerated, for 3 to 5 days.

Hearty Tomato Sauce

PREP TIME: 15 MINUTES • COOK TIME: 15 MINUTES AT HIGH PRESSURE, QUICK RELEASE

MAKES ABOUT 3½ CUPS This versatile sauce will quickly become your go-to topping for pasta dishes and pizza. Use good-quality tomatoes, such as imported ones like San Marzano or Pomi. If you start with whole tomatoes, chop them first. In the summer, I omit the dried basil and stir in 1 to 2 tablespoons of chopped fresh basil after the sauce is finished cooking. This sauce freezes well in zip-top freezer bags or plastic storage containers.

1. With the pressure cooker on the brown or sauté setting, heat the oil until it shimmers. Add the onion and sauté, stirring frequently, until the onion is softened and translucent, about 5 minutes. Add the garlic and sauté, stirring constantly, for 1 minute. Add the chopped tomatoes, tomato paste, oregano, basil, thyme, salt, and pepper. Stir to combine.

2. Lock on the lid and set the timer for 15 minutes at high pressure. When the timer goes off, quick release the pressure. Stir the sauce and use or store.

GLUTEN-FREE
SOY-FREE
NUT-FREE
VEGAN

2 tablespoons extra-virgin olive oil
* 1 onion, diced
* 2 garlic cloves, minced
* 1 (28-ounce) can whole or chopped tomatoes
* 2 tablespoons tomato paste
2 teaspoons dried oregano
1 teaspoon dried basil
½ teaspoon dried thyme
1 teaspoon kosher salt
⅛ teaspoon freshly ground black pepper

Preparation Tip *If you use whole tomatoes, chop them up by plunging a clean pair of kitchen shears into the open can and chopping up the tomatoes as finely as you like. They'll break down further during cooking.*

Balsamic White Bean Dip

PREP TIME: 10 MINUTES • COOK TIME: 25 MINUTES AT HIGH PRESSURE, NATURAL RELEASE

MAKES ABOUT 1 CUP Think of this dip as a sophisticated, Italian version of hummus. It can serve much the same purpose—use it as a dip for red peppers, endive, or celery, or slather it onto toasted bread. In particular, I like to serve it while it's still warm, which really allows the flavors of the roasted garlic to shine through. Fresh rosemary or parsley can be used in place of sage to change the flavors up a bit.

GLUTEN-FREE

SOY-FREE

NUT-FREE

VEGAN

* 8 ounces dried cannellini beans, rinsed
* 2 tablespoons roasted garlic purée
  2 tablespoons balsamic vinegar
  4 tablespoons extra-virgin olive oil, divided
* 1 tablespoon chopped fresh sage
  1 teaspoon kosher salt
  ⅛ teaspoon freshly ground black pepper

1. In the pot of a pressure cooker, add the beans and fill the pot with enough water to cover beans by about 2 inches.

2. Lock on the lid and set the timer for 25 minutes at high pressure. When the timer goes off, natural release the pressure for 10 minutes, then quick release any remaining pressure and remove the lid. Drain the beans in a colander, reserving about ¼ cup of the cooking liquid.

3. Transfer the beans to a food processor and pulse to begin puréeing the beans. Add the garlic, vinegar, 3 tablespoons of olive oil, sage, salt, and pepper. Continue puréeing until the dip is smooth and creamy. If the dip is too thick, add some of the reserved cooking liquid, 1 tablespoon at a time, as needed, to thin it out a bit. Transfer the dip to a serving dish and drizzle with the remaining 1 tablespoon of olive oil. The dip will keep, covered and refrigerated, for 3 to 5 days.

Garlicky Eggplant Dip

PREP TIME: 10 MINUTES ● COOK TIME: 4 MINUTES AT HIGH PRESSURE, QUICK RELEASE

MAKES ABOUT 2 CUPS This recipe is my take on baba ghanoush, a Middle Eastern dip made with eggplant. This spread is easy to make and great to serve at parties. Using prepared roasted garlic instead of the traditional fresh garlic gives it less of a pungent bite. The next time you have the impulse to buy those too-beautiful-to-resist newly harvested eggplants at the farmers' market, you'll know just what to do with them.

1. With the pressure cooker on the sauté or brown setting, heat 1 tablespoon of olive oil until it shimmers. Working in batches, place the eggplant pieces, cut-side down, in the hot oil and sear until it has browned, about 5 minutes. Remove the eggplant and set aside.

2. Add the vinegar to the pot and use a spatula or a wooden spoon to scrape up any browned bits on the bottom of the pot. Pour the water into the pot, then add the eggplant, stacking the pieces if necessary.

3. Lock on the lid and set the timer for 4 minutes at high pressure. When the timer goes off, quick release the pressure and remove the lid. Use tongs to remove the egg-plant, and set the pieces aside until they are cool enough to handle.

4. Scoop the flesh from the eggplant into a bowl and discard the eggplant skin. Stir in the garlic, lemon juice, tahini, remaining 1 tablespoon of olive oil, salt, and cay-enne pepper. If you want a smoother dip texture, use an immersion blender to purée the mixture or process it in a food processor. Serve warm or at room temperature. The eggplant spread will keep, tightly covered and refriger-ated, for up to 3 days.

GLUTEN-FREE SOY-FREE NUT-FREE VEGAN

- 2 tablespoons extra-virgin olive oil, divided
- 2 medium eggplant, halved, and each piece cut crosswise into 3 pieces
- 2 tablespoons white wine vinegar
- 1 cup water
- 1 tablespoon prepared roasted garlic
- 1 tablespoon freshly squeezed lemon juice
- 1 tablespoon tahini
- ½ teaspoon kosher salt, plus more as needed
- ½ teaspoon ground cayenne pepper

Ingredient Tip *If you don't have prepared roasted garlic, put 3 to 5 garlic cloves into the cooking liquid along with the egg-plant. Fish them out of the cooking liquid and mash them into the other ingredi-ents in step 4.*

Dumplings for Stews and Soups

PREP TIME: 10 MINUTES • COOK TIME: 2 MINUTES AT HIGH PRESSURE, QUICK RELEASE

MAKES 12 DUMPLINGS Dumplings are basically a version of biscuit dough that is cooked in a hot soup or stew liquid. In the liquid, they steam rather than bake, resulting in a fluffy, tender pastry. Add these dumplings to the Lentil-Mushroom Stew (page 111) or any other hearty stew.

SOY-FREE
NUT-FREE

2 cups all-purpose flour

1 teaspoon baking powder

¼ teaspoon kosher salt

6 tablespoons cold unsalted butter, cut into pieces

✳ ¾ cup buttermilk

✳ 2 tablespoons minced fresh parsley

1. In a large mixing bowl, whisk together the flour, baking powder, and salt. Add the cold butter and, using clean hands, work it into the dry ingredients until the butter pieces are pea-size. Add the buttermilk and use a fork to stir it into a shaggy dough. Stir in the parsley.

2. When the stew is finished cooking, drop the dumplings into the hot liquid by the spoonful. Let dumplings sit for a minute, then use a spoon to turn each dumpling over.

3. Lock on the lid and set the timer for 2 minutes at high pressure. When the timer goes off, quick release the pressure and remove the lid. Serve immediately.

Cheesy Cornbread

PREP TIME: 10 MINUTES • COOK TIME: 20 MINUTES AT HIGH PRESSURE, NATURAL RELEASE

SERVES 4 Make a batch of this hearty cornbread before you prepare one of the chili recipes in the One-Pot Wonders section. Cooked in a pressure cooker, this cornbread turns out dense and moist. If you like your cornbread with a touch of sweetness, stir a tablespoon of granulated sugar or honey into the batter. You can use the same method for a packaged cornbread mix if you adjust the ingredients needed as indicated by the instructions on the box.

SOY-FREE
NUT-FREE

Cooking spray

✹ 1 egg

✹ 1½ cups self-rising cornmeal

3 tablespoons unsalted butter, melted and slightly cooled

✹ ¾ cup whole milk

✹ ½ cup shredded Colby cheese

1 cup water

1. Spray a 7-inch round springform pan with the cooking spray. Set aside.

2. In a medium mixing bowl, whisk the egg. Stir in the cornmeal, then add the butter and milk and stir until the mixture is just combined. Fold the cheese into the batter, then spoon the batter into the prepared pan.

3. Place a rack or a steamer insert in the pressure cooker pot and add the water to the pot. Place the filled pan on the rack. Lock on the lid and set the timer for 20 minutes at high pressure. When the timer goes off, turn off the pressure cooker and natural release for 10 minutes. Quick release any remaining pressure, then remove the pan from the cooker. Remove the cornbread from the pan and cut it into wedges. Serve warm or at room temperature.

Ingredient Tip *To change up the flavors of this cornbread, try different cheeses. Pepper Jack or a sharp Cheddar cheese are both great choices. Also try stirring in ½ cup corn kernels (fresh or frozen thawed kernels) into the batter.*

Boiled Peanuts

PREP TIME: 5 MINUTES • COOK TIME: 1 HOUR AT HIGH PRESSURE, NATURAL RELEASE

SERVES 6 TO 8 When my friend Clay told me he uses his electric pressure cooker to make boiled peanuts, I was intrigued and he was nice enough to share his method. Boiled peanuts are a Southern treat, one you find at roadside stands and country fairs. The first time I tried them I was a little surprised that you eat them shell and all. Turns out the salty, chewy shell is the best part! Be sure to use raw peanuts, sometimes called green peanuts, not roasted ones. Some supermarkets keep them in the produce department.

1. Place the peanuts in the pressure cooker pot. Add water to the maximum fill line of the pressure cooker. Stir in the vegetable oil and salt.

2. Lock on the lid and set the timer for 1 hour at high pressure. When the timer goes off, natural release the pressure completely. Open the lid and use a slotted spoon to remove the peanuts from the cooking liquid. Serve hot or warm.

GLUTEN-FREE
SOY-FREE
VEGAN

* 1 pound raw (green) peanuts, in shells, rinsed
2 tablespoons vegetable oil
¼ cup kosher salt

Preparation Tip *Clay gives his peanuts a Cajun flavor by adding 2 teaspoons of ground red pepper and 2 teaspoons of granulated garlic to the pot before cooking.*

Quick Berry Compote

PREP TIME: 3 MINUTES • COOK TIME: 3 MINUTES AT HIGH PRESSURE, QUICK RELEASE

MAKES ABOUT 3 CUPS You'll find a dozen ways to enjoy this berry compote. It's a great recipe to make with extra fruit from a picking expedition, or simply to put together with a couple of bags of frozen fruit. The compote can be stirred into plain yogurt, spooned onto homemade French toast or waffles, topped on ice cream, or dolloped onto oatmeal. A little cornstarch gives it a thicker, syrupy consistency, making it more jam-like.

GLUTEN-FREE
SOY-FREE
NUT-FREE
VEGAN

* 4 cups fresh or frozen (thawed) berries
* 1 tablespoon freshly squeezed lemon juice
  ¼ cup granulated sugar
  ½ teaspoon cornstarch

1. Place the fruit in the pressure cooker pot. Sprinkle with the lemon juice, sugar, and cornstarch, and stir to combine.

2. Lock on the lid and set the timer for 3 minutes at high pressure. When the timer goes off, quick release the pressure and remove the lid. Stir the mixture. Let it cool slightly and serve warm, or cool completely and store, tightly covered, in the refrigerator for up to 2 weeks.

Old-Fashioned Applesauce

PREP TIME: 20 MINUTES • COOK TIME: 4 MINUTES AT HIGH PRESSURE, NATURAL RELEASE

MAKES ABOUT 4 CUPS While many pressure cooker instruction manuals advise against making applesauce in them (since the cooked apple mixture can splatter and potentially block the valves), I've never had any issues with this happening. Just be sure not to fill your cooker more than half full. A piece of parchment paper will help keep the apple from splattering. I like to eat my applesauce warm, spooned over a slab of gingerbread or pound cake.

GLUTEN-FREE
SOY-FREE
NUT-FREE
VEGAN

* 2½ pounds apples, peeled, cored, and cut into chunks
  ¼ cup brown sugar
* 1 teaspoon cinnamon
* ¾ cup apple juice or cider
* 1 tablespoon freshly squeezed lemon juice
  ⅛ teaspoon kosher salt

Ingredient Tip *The best apples for making applesauce are crisp, firm, and somewhat tart. Try Fuji, Gala, or Jonathan apples. You can also use a combination of apples; just make sure you have a balance of sweet and tart varieties.*

1. Cut out a round of parchment paper about ½ inch smaller than the circumference of your pressure cooker pot (trace the bottom edge of the pot as a guide). In the pressure cooker pot, combine the apples, brown sugar, cinnamon, apple juice, lemon juice, and salt. Place the parchment paper over the ingredients, gently pressing it down to moisten it.

2. Lock on the lid and set the timer for 4 minutes at high pressure. When the timer goes off, turn off or unplug the pressure cooker and natural release the pressure for 15 minutes, then quick release any remaining pressure. Open the lid and remove the parchment with tongs.

3. For a chunky applesauce, use a wooden spoon to stir the apples and break them into chunks. For a smoother consistency, transfer the mixture to a food processor or a food mill and process until smooth.

Spiced Vanilla Caramel Sauce

PREP TIME: 5 MINUTES • COOK TIME: 22 MINUTES AT HIGH PRESSURE, NATURAL RELEASE

MAKES ABOUT 1¾ CUPS I'd heard that sweetened condensed milk, still sealed in the can, can be simmered for hours on the stove to make thick caramel similar to the Latin treat dulce de leche. Turns out, unsurprisingly, that you can do it in even less time in the pressure cooker. Try using different extract flavors to change things up—almond or coffee would be luscious.

GLUTEN-FREE
SOY-FREE
NUT-FREE

- 1 (14-ounce) can sweetened condensed milk
- 1 teaspoon vanilla extract
- 1 teaspoon ground cinnamon
- 8 cups water
- 2 tablespoons unsalted butter

Serving Tip *This caramel is thick and spreadable. It makes a great filling between the layers of a cake or between sandwich cookies. If you want to drizzle it over ice cream, warm a couple of spoonfuls in a bowl in the microwave for 15 to 20 seconds.*

1. Spoon the sweetened condensed milk into a 16-ounce glass jar with a lid, such as a canning jar. Stir in the vanilla and cinnamon. Place the lid on the jar so that it is screwed closed just until it catches but is not tightened, and place it in the pressure cooker. Add the water to the pot; it should come about halfway up the side of the jar.

2. Lock the lid on the pressure cooker and set the timer for 22 minutes at high pressure. When the timer goes off, turn off or unplug the pressure cooker and natural release the pressure. When the pressure has been completely released, quick release any remaining pressure and open the pressure cooker lid.

3. Carefully remove the jar with an oven mitt, and let it cool slightly until it can be handled, 10 to 15 minutes. Open the lid and stir in the butter until the caramel is smooth and creamy. The caramel will keep for 2 weeks, covered and refrigerated.

Pumpkin Butter

PREP TIME: 10 MINUTES ● COOK TIME: 12 MINUTES AT HIGH PRESSURE, QUICK RELEASE

MAKES ABOUT 1¾ CUPS My post-college roommate, Lisa, used to make thick and delicious pumpkin butter every fall. We'd slather it on just about everything, from toast to cookies to butter crackers, even dipping apple slices in it. I adapted her version for the pressure cooker, which eliminates the need to constantly stir it. And it's made and ready to eat in far less time. It's a win all around.

1. In the pressure cooker pot, stir together the pumpkin purée, cider, brown sugar, spice, and salt.

2. Lock on the lid and set the timer for 12 minutes at high pressure. When the timer goes off, quick release the pressure and stir the mixture, scraping it off the bottom of the pot with a spatula. It should be thick, with a jammy consistency. Transfer the mixture to an airtight container and keep, refrigerated, for up to 1 week.

GLUTEN-FREE
SOY-FREE
NUT-FREE
VEGAN

* 1 can pumpkin purée
* ½ cup apple cider
   ½ cup dark brown sugar
   2 teaspoons pumpkin
      pie spice
   ⅛ teaspoon kosher salt

Ingredient Tip *If you don't have pumpkin spice mix, use 1 teaspoon ground cinnamon, ½ teaspoon ground ginger, and ¼ teaspoons each ground nutmeg and ground cloves.*

CONVERSION TABLES

VOLUME EQUIVALENTS (LIQUID)

US STANDARD	US STANDARD (OUNCES)	METRIC (APPROXIMATE)
2 tablespoons	1 fl. oz.	30 mL
¼ cup	2 fl. oz.	60 mL
½ cup	4 fl. oz.	120 mL
1 cup	8 fl. oz.	240 mL
1½ cups	12 fl. oz.	355 mL
2 cups or 1 pint	16 fl. oz.	475 mL
4 cups or 1 quart	32 fl. oz.	1 L
1 gallon	128 fl. oz.	4 L

OVEN TEMPERATURES

FAHRENHEIT (F)	CELSIUS (C) (APPROXIMATE)
250°F	120°C
300°F	150°C
325°F	165°C
350°F	180°C
375°F	190°C
400°F	200°C
425°F	220°C
450°F	230°C

VOLUME EQUIVALENTS (DRY)

US STANDARD	METRIC (APPROXIMATE)
¼ teaspoon	1 mL
½ teaspoon	2 mL
1 teaspoon	5 mL
1 tablespoon	15 mL
¼ cup	59 mL
⅓ cup	79 mL
½ cup	118 mL
1 cup	177 mL

WEIGHT EQUIVALENTS

US STANDARD	METRIC (APPROXIMATE)
½ ounce	15 g
1 ounce	30 g
2 ounces	60 g
4 ounces	115 g
8 ounces	225 g
12 ounces	340 g
16 ounces or 1 pound	455 g

REFERENCES

Corleone, Jill. "What Are the Health Benefits of Eating Pumpkin Puree." Updated January 11, 2014. Accessed November 7, 2016. www.livestrong.com/article/469900 -what-are-the-health-benefits-of-eating-pumpkin-puree.

Encyclopedia Britannica. "Denis Papin." *Encyclopedia Britannica*. Accessed November 4, 2016. www.britannica.com/biography/Denis-Papin.

Slazy, Jennifer. "Brown Rice: Health Benefits & Nutrition Facts." *Live Science*. April 11, 2015. Accessed November 7, 2016. www.livescience.com/50461-brown-rice -health-benefits-nutrition-facts.

Ware, Megan. "Chickpeas: Health Benefits, Nutritional Information." *Medical News Today*. Updated September 14, 2016. Accessed November 7, 2016. www .medicalnewstoday.com/articles/280244.php

RECIPE INDEX

A

Arugula Risotto, 86

B

Baked Eggs with Artichokes
   in Tomato Sauce, 97
Balsamic White Bean Dip, 138
Barbecue Beans, 48
Barley Bowl with Kale
   and Carrots, 37
Basic Black Beans, 40
Basic Brown Rice, 27
Basic Chickpeas, 42
Basic Pinto Beans, 41
Basic Quinoa, 32
Basic White Rice, 26
Beets, Two Ways, 60–61
Berry Cobbler, 122
Black Bean Soup with Chard
   and Veggie Sausage, 110
Boiled Peanuts, 142
Braised Red Cabbage, 66
Breakfast Custard for One, 77
Brown Rice with Scallions, 28
Brownie Pudding Cake, 132
Butter Beans with Tomatoes
   and Carrots, 49
Butternut Squash Soup with
   Coconut and Ginger, 107

C

Cardamom Rice Pudding, 130
Cheese Grits, 35
Cheesy Cauliflower Soup, 108
Cheesy Cornbread, 141
Cheesy Noodle "Helper," 98
Cider-Braised Brussels
   Sprouts, 68
Classic Chili, 115
Classic Polenta, 36
Corn Chowder, 112

Corn on the Cob,
   Four Ways, 67
Creamy Asparagus Soup, 102
Creamy Coconut Rice, 29
Cuban-Style Black Beans, 44

D

Dumplings for Stews
   and Soups, 140

F

Farro with Mushrooms
   and Walnuts, 31
French Onion Soup, 113
French Toast Casserole, 82–83

G

Garlicky Eggplant Dip, 139
Goat Cheese and Asparagus
   Breakfast Strata, 81
Green Beans, Four Ways, 58
Green Thai Tofu and
   Veggie Curry, 93

H

Harvest Ratatouille, 92
Hearty Tomato Sauce, 137
Herby Brown Rice Pilaf, 30
Herby Hummus, 136
Honey Stewed Figs with
   Goat Cheese, 125
Hoppin' John, 114

I

Indian Chickpea Curry, 94
Indian-Style Lentils, 43

K

Korean Sushi Bowls
   with Egg, 90

L

Leek and Asparagus
   Risotto, 88–89
Lemon Curd, 133
Lemon-Ricotta Cups, 126
Lentil-Mushroom Stew, 111

M

Maple-Glazed Carrots, 59
Moroccan Chickpea Stew, 103
Mushroom Soup, 105

N

New Potato Salad, 64

O

Old-Fashioned
   Applesauce, 144
Orange Crème Brûlée, 127

P

Parmesan Coddled Eggs, 75
Peas and Paneer in
   Indian Sauce, 99
Poached Eggs, 74
Pumpkin Bread Pudding, 131
Pumpkin Butter, 146
Pumpkin Oatmeal, 78

Q

Quick Berry Compote, 143
Quick Green Posole, 91
Quick Quinoa Chili, 116
Quinoa Porridge with
   Dried Fruit, 79
Quinoa, Tabbouleh Style, 33
Quinoa with Pine Nuts
   and Parmesan, 34

R

Red Wine Poached Pears, 123
Refried Beans, 47

Risotto with Peas, 87

Rosemary Potato-
Leek Soup, 109

Rosemary White Beans, 45

S

Seasoned Bok Choy, 55

Smoky Mashed Potatoes, 65

Soft-Cooked Egg on
Avocado Toast, 76

Spaghetti Squash with
Cheddar Cheese, 62

Spaghetti Squash with Pesto
and Fresh Mozzarella, 95

Speedy Scratch Mac
'n Cheese, 96

Spiced Vanilla Caramel
Sauce, 145

Spicy Kale, 56

Steamed Artichokes, 53

Steamed Asparagus,
Four Ways, 54

Steamed Broccoli or
Cauliflower, Four Ways, 52

Steel-Cut Oats with
Brown Sugar, Cinnamon,
and Almonds, 80

Stewed Collard Greens, 57

Stuffed Apples, 124

Sweet Potatoes with Ginger
and Cilantro, 63

T

Tomato Soup, Chunky
or Creamy, 104

Tortilla Soup, 106

Two-Bean Salad, 46

Two-Layer Cheesecake,
128–129

V

Vegetable Stock, 69

W

White Bean Chili, 117

INDEX

A

Almonds
  Steel-Cut Oats with
    Brown Sugar, Cinnamon,
    and Almonds, 80
Apples
  Old-Fashioned
    Applesauce, 144
  Stuffed Apples, 124
Artichokes
  Baked Eggs with
    Artichokes in
    Tomato Sauce, 97
  Steamed Artichokes, 53
Arugula
  Arugula Risotto, 86
Asparagus
  Creamy Asparagus
    Soup, 102
  Goat Cheese and
    Asparagus Breakfast
    Strata, 81
  Leek and Asparagus
    Risotto, 88–89
  Steamed Asparagus,
    Four Ways, 54
Avocados
  Korean Sushi Bowls
    with Egg, 90
  Soft-Cooked Egg on
    Avocado Toast, 76

B

Barley
  Barley Bowl with Kale
    and Carrots, 37
Beans. *See also* Black beans;
  Black-eyed peas; Cannellini
  beans; Chickpeas; Green
  beans; Kidney beans;
  Lentils; Lima beans; Navy
  beans; Pinto beans

cook times, 19
  soaking vs. dry
    method, 11–12
Beets
  Beets, Two Ways, 60–61
Bell peppers
  Cuban-Style Black
    Beans, 44
  Green Thai Tofu and
    Veggie Curry, 93
  Harvest Ratatouille, 92
  Hoppin' John, 114
Berries
  Berry Cobbler, 122
  Quick Berry Compote, 143
Black beans
  Basic Black Beans, 40
  Black Bean Soup with
    Chard and Veggie
    Sausage, 110
  Cuban-Style Black
    Beans, 44
  Two-Bean Salad, 46
Black-eyed peas
  Hoppin' John, 114
Bok choy
  Seasoned Bok Choy, 55
Bread
  Baked Eggs with
    Artichokes in
    Tomato Sauce, 97
  French Onion Soup, 113
  French Toast
    Casserole, 82–83
  Goat Cheese and
    Asparagus Breakfast
    Strata, 81
  Pumpkin Bread
    Pudding, 131
  Soft-Cooked Egg on
    Avocado Toast, 76

Broccoli
  Steamed Broccoli
    or Cauliflower,
    Four Ways, 52
Brown function, 12
Brussels sprouts
  Cider-Braised Brussels
    Sprouts, 68
Butternut squash
  Butternut Squash
    Soup with Coconut
    and Ginger, 107

C

Cabbage
  Braised Red Cabbage, 66
Cannellini beans
  Balsamic White
    Bean Dip, 138
  Rosemary White Beans, 45
Carrots
  Barley Bowl with Kale
    and Carrots, 37
  Butter Beans with
    Tomatoes and
    Carrots, 49
  Indian Chickpea Curry, 94
  Lentil-Mushroom Stew, 111
  Maple-Glazed Carrots, 59
  Moroccan Chickpea
    Stew, 103
  Vegetable Stock, 69
Cauliflower
  Cheesy Cauliflower
    Soup, 108
  Steamed Broccoli
    or Cauliflower,
    Four Ways, 52
Celery
  Hoppin' John, 114
  New Potato Salad, 64
  Vegetable Stock, 69

Chard
    Black Bean Soup with
        Chard and Veggie
        Sausage, 110
Cheddar cheese
    Breakfast Custard
        for One, 77
    Cheese Grits, 35
    Cheesy Noodle
        "Helper," 98
    Spaghetti Squash with
        Cheddar Cheese, 62
    Speedy Scratch Mac
        'n Cheese, 96
Cheese. *See* Cheddar cheese;
    Colby cheese; Cream cheese;
    Goat cheese; Gruyère
    cheese; Mozzarella cheese;
    Paneer cheese; Parmesan
    cheese; Ricotta cheese
Chickpeas
    Basic Chickpeas, 42
    Herby Hummus, 136
    Indian Chickpea Curry, 94
    Moroccan Chickpea
        Stew, 103
Chocolate. *See* Cocoa powder
Cilantro
    Peas and Paneer in
        Indian Sauce, 99
    Sweet Potatoes with
        Ginger and Cilantro, 63
    Two-Bean Salad, 46
Cocoa powder
    Brownie Pudding Cake, 132
Coconut milk
    Butternut Squash
        Soup with Coconut
        and Ginger, 107
    Creamy Coconut Rice, 29
    Indian Chickpea Curry, 94
Colby cheese
    Cheesy Cornbread, 141
Collard greens
    Stewed Collard Greens, 57

Cooking times, 10
Corn. *See also* Cornmeal;
    Grits; Hominy; Polenta
    Classic Chili, 115
    Corn Chowder, 112
    Corn on the Cob,
        Four Ways, 67
    Quick Quinoa Chili, 116
    Tortilla Soup, 106
    Two-Bean Salad, 46
Cornmeal. *See also* Polenta
    Cheesy Cornbread, 141
Cream cheese
    Two-Layer Cheesecake,
        128–129

D
Dicing, 16

E
Eggplant
    Garlicky Eggplant Dip, 139
    Harvest Ratatouille, 92
Eggs
    Baked Eggs with
        Artichokes in
        Tomato Sauce, 97
    cook times, 20
    Korean Sushi Bowls
        with Egg, 90
    Lemon Curd, 133
    Orange Crème Brûlée, 127
    Parmesan Coddled
        Eggs, 75
    Poached Eggs, 74
    Soft-Cooked Egg on
        Avocado Toast, 76
Equipment, 16

F
Farro
    Farro with Mushrooms
        and Walnuts, 31
Figs
    Honey Stewed Figs with
        Goat Cheese, 125

Fruits. *See also specific*
    Quinoa Porridge with
        Dried Fruit, 79

G
Ginger
    Butternut Squash
        Soup with Coconut
        and Ginger, 107
    Sweet Potatoes with
        Ginger and Cilantro, 63
Goat cheese
    Goat Cheese and
        Asparagus Breakfast
        Strata, 81
    Honey Stewed Figs with
        Goat Cheese, 125
Grains. *See also* Barley;
    Farro; Oats; Quinoa; Rice
    cook times, 19
Great northern beans
    White Bean Chili, 117
Green beans
    Green Beans, Four
        Ways, 58
    Green Thai Tofu and
        Veggie Curry, 93
Greens. *See* Arugula;
    Bok choy; Chard;
    Collard greens; Kale
Grits
    Cheese Grits, 35
Gruyère cheese
    Cheesy Cauliflower
        Soup, 108
    French Onion Soup, 113

H
Hominy. *See also* Grits
    Quick Green Posole, 91

I
Ingredients
    basic, 9
    prepping, 16–17
    spices, 10

J

Jalapeños
    Quick Green Posole, 91
Julienning, 16

K

Kale
    Barley Bowl with Kale
      and Carrots, 37
    Spicy Kale, 56
Kidney beans
    Classic Chili, 115
    Quick Quinoa Chili, 116
    Two-Bean Salad, 46
Knife skills, 16

L

Leeks
    Leek and Asparagus
      Risotto, 88–89
    Mushroom Soup, 105
    Rosemary Potato-
      Leek Soup, 109
Legumes. See Beans
Lemons
    Lemon Curd, 133
    Lemon-Ricotta Cups, 126
Lentils
    Indian-Style Lentils, 43
    Lentil-Mushroom Stew, 111
Lima beans
    Butter Beans with
      Tomatoes and
      Carrots, 49

M

Meatless crumbles
    Cheesy Noodle
      "Helper," 98
    White Bean Chili, 117
Meatless sausage
    Black Bean Soup with
      Chard and Veggie
      Sausage, 110
Mincing, 16
Mozzarella cheese

Spaghetti Squash with
    Pesto and Fresh
    Mozzarella, 95
Mushrooms
    Farro with Mushrooms
      and Walnuts, 31
    Lentil-Mushroom Stew, 111
    Mushroom Soup, 105

N

Natural release, 13
Navy beans
    Barbecue Beans, 48
Nuts. See Almonds; Peanuts;
  Pine nuts; Walnuts

O

Oats
    Berry Cobbler, 122
    Pumpkin Oatmeal, 78
    Steel-Cut Oats with
      Brown Sugar, Cinnamon,
      and Almonds, 80
    Stuffed Apples, 124
Onions
    French Onion Soup, 113

P

Paneer cheese
    Peas and Paneer in
      Indian Sauce, 99
Parmesan cheese
    Arugula Risotto, 86
    Baked Eggs with
      Artichokes in
      Tomato Sauce, 97
    Barley Bowl with Kale
      and Carrots, 37
    Classic Polenta, 36
    Leek and Asparagus
      Risotto, 88–89
    Parmesan Coddled
      Eggs, 75
    Quinoa with Pine Nuts
      and Parmesan, 34
    Risotto with Peas, 87

Pasta
    Cheesy Noodle
      "Helper," 98
    Speedy Scratch Mac
      'n Cheese, 96
Peanuts
    Boiled Peanuts, 142
Pears
    Red Wine Poached
      Pears, 123
Peas
    Peas and Paneer in
      Indian Sauce, 99
    Risotto with Peas, 87
Peppers. See Bell
  peppers; Jalapeños
Pine nuts
    Quinoa with Pine Nuts
      and Parmesan, 34
Pinto beans
    Basic Pinto Beans, 41
    Refried Beans, 47
Polenta
    Classic Polenta, 36
Potatoes. See also
  Sweet potatoes
    Corn Chowder, 112
    New Potato Salad, 64
    Rosemary Potato-
      Leek Soup, 109
    Smoky Mashed
      Potatoes, 65
Pounds per square
  inch (psi), 12
Prepping, 16–17
Pressure cookers
    best foods for, 10–11
    cleaning and care, 14
    cook times, 18–21
    dos and don'ts, 14–15
    history of, 9
    releasing pressure, 13
    settings, 12
Pumpkin
    Pumpkin Bread
      Pudding, 131

Pumpkin Butter, 146
Pumpkin Oatmeal, 78

Q

Quick release, 13
Quinoa
    Basic Quinoa, 32
    Quick Quinoa Chili, 116
    Quinoa Porridge with
        Dried Fruit, 79
    Quinoa, Tabbouleh
        Style, 33
    Quinoa with Pine Nuts
        and Parmesan, 34

R

Raisins
    Pumpkin Bread
        Pudding, 131
    Stuffed Apples, 124
Rice
    Arugula Risotto, 86
    Basic Brown Rice, 27
    Basic White Rice, 26
    Brown Rice with
        Scallions, 28
    Cardamom Rice
        Pudding, 130
    cook times, 18
    Creamy Coconut Rice, 29
    Herby Brown Rice
        Pilaf, 30
    Korean Sushi Bowls
        with Egg, 90
    Leek and Asparagus
        Risotto, 88–89
    Risotto with Peas, 87
Ricotta cheese
    Lemon-Ricotta Cups, 126

S

Safety, 13
Scallions
    Brown Rice with
        Scallions, 28
Shallots
    Arugula Risotto, 86
    Cider-Braised Brussels
        Sprouts, 68
    Creamy Asparagus
        Soup, 102
    Farro with Mushrooms
        and Walnuts, 31
    Risotto with Peas, 87
Spaghetti squash
    Spaghetti Squash with
        Cheddar Cheese, 62
    Spaghetti Squash with
        Pesto and Fresh
        Mozzarella, 95
Squash. See Butternut
    squash; Spaghetti
    squash; Yellow squash
Sweet potatoes
    Sweet Potatoes with
        Ginger and Cilantro, 63

T

Tofu
    Green Thai Tofu and
        Veggie Curry, 93
Tomatillos
    Quick Green Posole, 91
Tomatoes
    Butter Beans with
        Tomatoes and
        Carrots, 49

Cheesy Noodle
    "Helper," 98
Classic Chili, 115
Harvest Ratatouille, 92
Hearty Tomato Sauce, 137
Moroccan Chickpea
    Stew, 103
Quick Quinoa Chili, 116
Quinoa, Tabbouleh
    Style, 33
Rosemary White Beans, 45
Spaghetti Squash with
    Pesto and Fresh
    Mozzarella, 95
Tomato Soup, Chunky
    or Creamy, 104
Tortilla Soup, 106

V

Vegetables. See also specific
    cook times, 20–21

W

Walnuts
    Farro with Mushrooms
        and Walnuts, 31
White beans. See Cannellini
    beans; Great northern
    beans; Navy beans

Y

Yellow squash
    Harvest Ratatouille, 92

RECIPE LABEL INDEX

Gluten-free

Arugula Risotto, 86

Baked Eggs with Artichokes in Tomato Sauce, 97

Balsamic White Bean Dip, 138

Barley Bowl with Kale and Carrots, 37

Basic Black Beans, 40

Basic Brown Rice, 27

Basic Chickpeas, 42

Basic Pinto Beans, 41

Basic Quinoa, 32

Basic White Rice, 26

Beets, Two Ways, 60–61

Boiled Peanuts, 142

Braised Red Cabbage, 66

Butter Beans with Tomatoes and Carrots, 49

Butternut Squash Soup with Coconut and Ginger, 107

Cardamom Rice Pudding, 130

Cheese Grits, 35

Cider-Braised Brussels Sprouts, 68

Classic Chili, 115

Classic Polenta, 36

Corn Chowder, 112

Corn on the Cob, Four Ways, 67

Creamy Asparagus Soup, 102

Creamy Coconut Rice, 29

Cuban-Style Black Beans, 44

Garlicky Eggplant Dip, 139

Green Beans, Four Ways, 58

Green Thai Tofu and Veggie Curry, 93

Harvest Ratatouille, 92

Hearty Tomato Sauce, 137

Herby Brown Rice Pilaf, 30

Herby Hummus, 136

Honey Stewed Figs with Goat Cheese, 125

Hoppin' John, 114

Indian Chickpea Curry, 94

Indian-Style Lentils, 43

Korean Sushi Bowls with Egg, 90

Leek and Asparagus Risotto, 88–89

Lemon Curd, 133

Lentil-Mushroom Stew, 111

Maple-Glazed Carrots, 59

Moroccan Chickpea Stew, 103

New Potato Salad, 64

Old-Fashioned Applesauce, 144

Orange Crème Brûlée, 127

Parmesan Coddled Eggs, 75

Peas and Paneer in Indian Sauce, 99

Poached Eggs, 74

Pumpkin Butter, 146

Pumpkin Oatmeal, 78

Quick Berry Compote, 143

Quick Green Posole, 91

Quick Quinoa Chili, 116

Quinoa Porridge with Dried Fruit, 79

Quinoa, Tabbouleh Style, 33

Quinoa with Pine Nuts and Parmesan, 34

Red Wine Poached Pears, 123

Refried Beans, 47

Risotto with Peas, 87

Rosemary Potato-Leek Soup, 109

Rosemary White Beans, 45

Smoky Mashed Potatoes, 65

Spaghetti Squash with Cheddar Cheese, 62

Spaghetti Squash with Pesto and Fresh Mozzarella, 95

Spiced Vanilla Caramel Sauce, 145

Spicy Kale, 56

Steamed Artichokes, 53

Steamed Asparagus, Four Ways, 54

Steel-Cut Oats with Brown Sugar, Cinnamon, and Almonds, 80

Stewed Collard Greens, 57

Stuffed Apples, 124

Sweet Potatoes with Ginger and Cilantro, 63

Tomato Soup, Chunky or Creamy, 104

Tortilla Soup, 106

Two-Bean Salad, 46

Vegetable Stock, 69

Nut-free

Arugula Risotto, 86

Baked Eggs with Artichokes in Tomato Sauce, 97

Balsamic White Bean Dip, 138

Barbecue Beans, 48

Barley Bowl with Kale and Carrots, 37

Basic Black Beans, 40

Basic Brown Rice, 27

Basic Chickpeas, 42

Basic Pinto Beans, 41

Basic Quinoa, 32

Basic White Rice, 26

Beets, Two Ways, 60–61

Berry Cobbler, 122

Black Bean Soup with Chard and Veggie Sausage, 110

Braised Red Cabbage, 66

Breakfast Custard for One, 77

Brown Rice with Scallions, 28

Brownie Pudding Cake, 132

Butter Beans with Tomatoes and Carrots, 49

Butternut Squash Soup with Coconut and Ginger, 107

Cardamom Rice Pudding, 130

Cheese Grits, 35

Cheesy Cauliflower Soup, 108

Cheesy Cornbread, 141

Cheesy Noodle "Helper," 98

Cider-Braised Brussels Sprouts, 68

Classic Chili, 115

Classic Polenta, 36

Corn Chowder, 112

Corn on the Cob, Four Ways, 67

Creamy Asparagus Soup, 102

Creamy Coconut Rice, 29

Cuban-Style Black Beans, 44

Dumplings for Stews and Soups, 140

French Onion Soup, 113

French Toast Casserole, 82–83

Garlicky Eggplant Dip, 139

Goat Cheese and Asparagus Breakfast Strata, 81

Green Thai Tofu and Veggie Curry, 93

Harvest Ratatouille, 92

Hearty Tomato Sauce, 137

Herby Brown Rice Pilaf, 30

Herby Hummus, 136

Honey Stewed Figs with Goat Cheese, 125

Hoppin' John, 114

Indian Chickpea Curry, 94

Indian-Style Lentils, 43

Korean Sushi Bowls with Egg, 90

Leek and Asparagus Risotto, 88–89

Lemon Curd, 133

Lemon-Ricotta Cups, 126

Lentil-Mushroom Stew, 111

Maple-Glazed Carrots, 59

Moroccan Chickpea Stew, 103

Mushroom Soup, 105

New Potato Salad, 64

Old-Fashioned Applesauce, 144

Orange Crème Brûlée, 127

Parmesan Coddled Eggs, 75

Peas and Paneer in Indian Sauce, 99

Poached Eggs, 74

Pumpkin Bread Pudding, 131

Pumpkin Butter, 146

Pumpkin Oatmeal, 78

Quick Berry Compote, 143

Quick Green Posole, 91

Quick Quinoa Chili, 116

Quinoa Porridge with Dried Fruit, 79

Quinoa, Tabbouleh Style, 33

Red Wine Poached Pears, 123

Refried Beans, 47

Risotto with Peas, 87

Rosemary Potato-Leek Soup, 109

Rosemary White Beans, 45

Seasoned Bok Choy, 55

Smoky Mashed Potatoes, 65

Soft-Cooked Egg on Avocado Toast, 76

Spaghetti Squash with Cheddar Cheese, 62

Speedy Scratch Mac 'n Cheese, 96

Spiced Vanilla Caramel Sauce, 145

Spicy Kale, 56

Steamed Artichokes, 53

Steamed Broccoli or Cauliflower, Four Ways, 52

Stewed Collard Greens, 57

Stuffed Apples, 124

Sweet Potatoes with Ginger and Cilantro, 63

Tomato Soup, Chunky or Creamy, 104

Tortilla Soup, 106

Two-Bean Salad, 46

Two-Layer Cheesecake, 128–129

Vegetable Stock, 69

White Bean Chili, 117

Soy-free

Arugula Risotto, 86

Baked Eggs with Artichokes in Tomato Sauce, 97

Balsamic White Bean Dip, 138

Barley Bowl with Kale and Carrots, 37

Basic Black Beans, 40

Basic Brown Rice, 27

Basic Chickpeas, 42

Basic Pinto Beans, 41

Basic Quinoa, 32

Basic White Rice, 26

Beets, Two Ways, 60–61

Berry Cobbler, 122

Boiled Peanuts, 142

Braised Red Cabbage, 66

Breakfast Custard for One, 77

Brownie Pudding Cake, 132

Butter Beans with Tomatoes and Carrots, 49

Butternut Squash Soup with Coconut and Ginger, 107

Cardamom Rice Pudding, 130

Cheese Grits, 35

Cheesy Cauliflower Soup, 108

Cheesy Cornbread, 141

Cider-Braised Brussels Sprouts, 68

Classic Chili, 115

Classic Polenta, 36

Corn on the Cob, Four Ways, 67

Creamy Asparagus Soup, 102

Creamy Coconut Rice, 29

Cuban-Style Black Beans, 44

Dumplings for Stews and Soups, 140

Farro with Mushrooms and Walnuts, 31

French Toast Casserole, 82–83

Garlicky Eggplant Dip, 139

Goat Cheese and Asparagus Breakfast Strata, 81

Harvest Ratatouille, 92

Hearty Tomato Sauce, 137

Herby Brown Rice Pilaf, 30

Herby Hummus, 136

Honey Stewed Figs with Goat Cheese, 125

Hoppin' John, 114

Indian Chickpea Curry, 94

Indian-Style Lentils, 43

Leek and Asparagus Risotto, 88–89

Lemon Curd, 133

Lemon-Ricotta Cups, 126

Maple-Glazed Carrots, 59

Moroccan Chickpea Stew, 103

Mushroom Soup, 105

Old-Fashioned Applesauce, 144

Orange Crème Brûlée, 127

Parmesan Coddled Eggs, 75

Peas and Paneer in Indian Sauce, 99

Poached Eggs, 74

Pumpkin Bread Pudding, 131

Pumpkin Butter, 146

Pumpkin Oatmeal, 78

Quick Berry Compote, 143

Quick Green Posole, 91

Quick Quinoa Chili, 116

Quinoa Porridge with Dried Fruit, 79

Quinoa, Tabbouleh Style, 33

Quinoa with Pine Nuts and Parmesan, 34

Red Wine Poached Pears, 123

Refried Beans, 47

Risotto with Peas, 87

Rosemary Potato-Leek Soup, 109

Rosemary White Beans, 45

Smoky Mashed Potatoes, 65

Soft-Cooked Egg on Avocado Toast, 76

Spaghetti Squash with Cheddar Cheese, 62

Spaghetti Squash with Pesto and Fresh Mozzarella, 95

Speedy Scratch Mac 'n Cheese, 96

Spiced Vanilla Caramel Sauce, 145

Spicy Kale, 56

Steamed Artichokes, 53

Steamed Asparagus, Four Ways, 54

Steamed Broccoli or Cauliflower, Four Ways, 52

Steel-Cut Oats with Brown Sugar, Cinnamon, and Almonds, 80

Stewed Collard Greens, 57

Stuffed Apples, 124

Sweet Potatoes with Ginger and Cilantro, 63

Tomato Soup, Chunky or Creamy, 104

Tortilla Soup, 106

Two-Bean Salad, 46

Two-Layer Cheesecake, 128–129

Vegetable Stock, 69

Vegan

Balsamic White Bean Dip, 138

Barbecue Beans, 48

Basic Black Beans, 40

Basic Brown Rice, 27

Basic Chickpeas, 42

Basic Pinto Beans, 41

Basic Quinoa, 32

Basic White Rice, 26

Black Bean Soup with Chard and Veggie Sausage, 110

Boiled Peanuts, 142

Brown Rice with Scallions, 28

Butter Beans with Tomatoes and Carrots, 49

Butternut Squash Soup with Coconut and Ginger, 107

Cider-Braised Brussels Sprouts, 68

Classic Chili, 115

Creamy Coconut Rice, 29

Cuban-Style Black Beans, 44

Farro with Mushrooms and Walnuts, 31

Garlicky Eggplant Dip, 139

Green Thai Tofu and Veggie Curry, 93

Harvest Ratatouille, 92

Hearty Tomato Sauce, 137

Herby Brown Rice Pilaf, 30

Hoppin' John, 114

Indian Chickpea Curry, 94

Indian-Style Lentils, 43

Moroccan Chickpea Stew, 103

Old-Fashioned Applesauce, 144

Pumpkin Butter, 146

Quick Berry Compote, 143

Quick Green Posole, 91

Quick Quinoa Chili, 116

Quinoa, Tabbouleh Style, 33

Red Wine Poached Pears, 123

Refried Beans, 47

Rosemary White Beans, 45

Seasoned Bok Choy, 55

Spicy Kale, 56

Steamed Artichokes, 53

Stewed Collard Greens, 57

Sweet Potatoes with Ginger and Cilantro, 63

Tortilla Soup, 106

Two-Bean Salad, 46

Vegetable Stock, 69

ABOUT THE AUTHOR

Jessica Goldbogen Harlan first discovered the joy of cooking when she enrolled in the Institute of Culinary Education in New York City. A longtime food writer, her byline has appeared in *Clean Eating, Pilates Style, Village Voice, About.com, Arthritis Today, Town & Country*, and more. She is also a caterer and culinary instructor for both kids and adults. She lives in Atlanta with her husband and two daughters. This is her seventh cookbook.

CPSIA information can be obtained
at www.ICGtesting.com
Printed in the USA
BVOW11s2000030317
477432BV00001B/1/P